THE POWER OF COACHING

MANAGING THE TIME OF YOUR LIFE

By

Machen MacDonald

With Co-Authors:

- Ruben Gonzalez
- Harry P. Hoopis
- Jose Feliciano
- Brian Tracy
- Stephen R. Covey
- Scott Taylor
- Alison Arnold
- Diane M. Ruebling
- Jim Rohn
- Denis Waitley
- Germaine Porché
- Jed Niederer
- Debra J. Satterwhite
- Jim Rohn

The Power of Coaching
Managing the Time of Your Life
Published by PLI Publishing
www.ThePowerOfCoaching.com
530-273-8000
Grass Valley, California

Copyright © 2008 ProBrilliance Leadership Institute (PLI)
Library of Congress Control Number: 2008901437
ISBN: 978-1-60585-394-9

Cover Design by Taylor Made Marketing
scott@fastpathcoaching.com

Editing, Composition, and Typography by Patti McKenna
PCMCKENNA6@aol.com

This book is available at quantity discounts for bulk purchase.
For more information, contact:
www.ThePowerOfCoaching.com
Telephone: 530-273-8000
Grass Valley, California

Printed in the United States of America

WHAT OTHERS ARE SAYING ABOUT THE POWER OF COACHING... MANAGING THE TIME OF YOUR LIFE!

"Managing the TIME of Your Life will help readers organize their time and prioritize their activities to achieve extraordinary results in every area of their lives – on the job, at home, and in their communities."

--Edward G. Deutschlander, CLU, CLF
Executive Vice President
North Star Resource Group
www.northstarfinancial.com

"If you are looking for simple, yet effective, strategies to become a better coach in getting your team and clients to accomplish more, then this book is a must read."

--Lou Cassara, CLU ChFC
CEO and Founder
The Cassara Clinic LLC
www.cassaraclinic.com

"Opportunities come upon us every day... only a few can see them and even less know what to do with them. The Power of Coaching coaches you to see the opportunities and know what to do with them."

--Seth A. Radow
Senior Vice President - Investments/Chairman's Club Member
UBS Financial Services

"Managing The TIME of Your Life should be required reading for everyone in a leadership position."

--Eric Lofholm
President and CEO
Eric Lofholm International, Inc
www.ericlofholm.com

"Machen MacDonald continues to capture the brilliance in others and invest it back for all to utilize. His and others' contributions to his latest compilation of best practices thinking will enrich your capacity to accelerate your leadership readiness and those around you." **--Jeff Hughes**
CEO GAMA International
GAMA: Building the Leaders Who
Build the Financial Services Industry
www.gamaweb.com

"Managing the TIME of Your Life is a powerful book in The Power of Coaching book series. It is full of practical ways and great perspectives to develop the crucial and important skill of coaching people to get more done in less time."

--Kent M. Campbell
Exec VP of Sales and Distribution
AvivaUsa

ACKNOWLEDGEMENTS

To my family for living the brilliant life! You make it all worthwhile and fun!

To **Patti McKenna** for your professional editing and doing such a wonderful job of bringing this project together with such ease.

To **Scott Taylor** for your creative genius and follow through—another fantastic book to your credit.

To **Jose Feliciano** for living an exemplary life filled with "make it happen" power and allowing me to be part of your world. I appreciate you and our friendship.

To **Jed Niederer** and **Germaine Porche'** for your contribution to the coaching world through the brilliance of your humor and the wisdom of your insights.

To **Diane Ruebling** for your friendship and professional support. It is a gift to work with you on our many projects. The time is right for leaders to get REAL through dynamic performance systems, and you are the one to lead it.

To **Harry Hoopis** for your incredible insights and ability to take the complex and simplify it so that so many can benefit and thereby live an inspiring life of service and contribution.

To **Stephen Covey** for your contribution of providing balance along the way of achievement. Your wise insights and awareness are astounding.

To **Doc Ali** for your playfulness and ability to motivate and inspire. You impact so many in such a great way at the perfect time. Keep living the dream.

To **Dr. Denis Waitley** for sharing your articulation of such deep knowledge of the human psychology and for showing people how to live a fuller life.

To **Ruben Gonzalez** for never, never, never quitting and being the "Bull Dog." Your commitment and enthusiasm are absolutely contagious, and it is so cool to see you affect people so deeply.

To **Deb Satterwhite** for our monthly breakfasts to dive in and bring to life the great ideas that are percolating in us all. You are on purpose, girl!

To **Brian Tracy** for your incredibly inspiring messages of leadership and achievement.

To **Jim Rohn** for your direct and perceptive acumen to help others raise the bar and win their game.

To **God** for all that is, was, and ever will be.

TABLE OF CONTENTS

FOREWORD
By Three-Time Olympian
Ruben Gonzalez

Would you like to be able to reach your goals in half the time? Would you like to have a greater sense of control over your life?

People who have a sense of control over their lives are happier and more confident than people who feel out of control. A big part of achieving that sense of control is learning how to manage your time.

That's why I'm excited about Machen MacDonald's new book, "The Power of Coaching...Managing the TIME of Your Life." Machen has brought together a group of time management experts who will show you how to take advantage of your time so you can be more effective in whatever you do. What I like best about this book is that its principles will work for anyone—whether you're an insurance agent, a financial planner, a banker, a stock broker, or... even an athlete, like me.

I competed in three Winter Olympics in the sport of luge over a period of three decades. Today, I speak professionally around the world about how to become unstoppable on the way to reaching your goals. Whether I'm speaking to 25 people in the boardroom of a Fortune 100 bank or to 6,500 insurance agents at the Million Dollar Round Table, I always say that I never would have made it to the Olympics without a coach, and I never would have made it if I could not manage my time.

Machen MacDonald is an incredible corporate coach. He gets results. Period. In this gem of a book, he shares his knowledge and the knowledge of his expert friends to help you reach your goals in record time.

You'll learn how to manage your time, but, in actuality, you will not be managing time. You will be managing yourself so you can take maximum advantage of your time. After all, you really can't manage time. Time keeps on moving forward, and there's nothing we can do about it. What you will be doing is setting priorities and focusing on YOUR priorities.

You'll learn to start saying "NO" to anything that will keep you from achieving your goals. You'll start focusing single-mindedly on your desired end result, and you will be amazed at how much you achieve in your life.

Read this book, highlight it, write notes all over it, re-read it, master its universal principles of success, and you will become unstoppable on the way to your goals and dreams.

Ruben Gonzalez
Olympian, Author, Keynote Speaker
www.TheOlympicSpeaker.com

INTRODUCTION

Time is of the essence in this book.

If you are familiar with "The Power of Coaching" book series, you have come to know these books serve as a resource for you, the leader, to more proficiently coach the people you lead. If this is your first exposure to "The Power of Coaching" series, you have attracted into your hands a powerful tool in raising your game and the game of the people for whom you are aligned to inspire, motivate, and propel to their potential.

In coaching leaders of many different sales organizations, I notice there always seems to be a common theme at the core of most bottlenecks, plateaus, and dysfunctions. The element is what people refer to as time management. However, rather than call it time management, I choose to address it as managing ourselves in relation to time. The reality is we can no more manage time than we can manage gravity or the weather. What we can manage is ourselves and the people we lead and coach in relation to this force known as time. Let's face it...there is always going to be more to do than we can do, and the bar is only going to continue to rise. To that point, this book is dedicated to you, the corporate athlete who is on the front line and responsible for leading the people to make it happen—to you, who must get results and make it happen. For without you, the organization comes to a grinding halt. Share values plummet. Resources dry up. You are the life force that allows and provides increase and expansion, all of which are good.

The majority of people are under the hallucination that we live in the information age. It has been brought to my attention that we are well beyond that. We now live in the age of attention. In order to thrive, not just survive, we must be conscious of what information we allow in and direct our attention toward. The information and data that floods us is either contributing to our energy level or contaminating it. In order to continue to be effective, productive, and stay on purpose, it must become our mission to manage our attention in relation to time. What is our vision? What data, info, intelligence, and wisdom are coming at us? What does all that mean to us? And, what do we do with it? These are the leading questions we must have the answers to within nanoseconds of each other if we are to steer clear of overwhelm.

It is said that the quality of our life is in direct proportion to our ability to handle uncertainty. Uncertainty is really just misunderstanding time in the sense of not being in the present moment and either regretting the past or worrying about the future. The past and future are not real. The past is gone, and the future has not happened yet. Therefore, the only real way to gain back our power is to be present.

As with the other books in "The Power of Coaching" series, this is an anthology. In addition to me, you will experience the wisdom of other business coaches and business leaders who have mastered the art of managing themselves effectively in relation to time. They have the mindset and skill set to coach others to manage themselves in relation to time. You will thereby gain different perspectives on becoming more effective. You may notice that some of the authors share what appears to be similar viewpoints and perspectives. This is done with intention. Hearing the same message said in a different way often lends itself to deepening one's learning.

This book is not about the newest or latest craze. It is about learning, understanding, and mastering proven principles. This is your resource for getting things done in a timely manner through yourself and others.

Some of the messages provide 'how to' and methodology for enhanced skill set, while others are about establishing superior mindset and perspective. It is our intent that together these will serve you in improving your coaching skills to help those you lead live more successful and fulfilling lives, while allowing you to do the same.

Underline what strikes you as useful. Dog ear the pages that contain common themes which present themselves in your daily life for easy future reference. Share what you learn and deepen your learning while serving others.

Finally, congratulations on affecting others so profoundly, and thank you for allowing us to share our insights that may help in that continued endeavor. Here's to *Provoking Your Brilliance* and to you provoking the brilliance of others!

Just in time,
Machen MacDonald

"Don't be fooled by the calendar.
There are only as many days in the year as
you make use of. One man gets only a week's
value out of a year,
while another man gets a
full year's value out of a week."

– Charles Richards

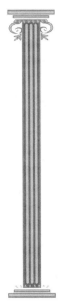**Machen MacDonald, CPCC, CCSC** is the creator of "The Power of Coaching" book series, the founder of the ProBrilliance Leadership Institute, and a full-time certified business and personal coach. With over 15 years of experience in the financial services industry, he's now a full-time coach dedicated to showing business leaders how to provoke their brilliance so they can experience their ideal life. He's an accomplished author, as well as a highly sought after speaker for his dynamic and unique perspectives on achieving success in all areas of life. Machen resides on his ranch in Northern California with his wife and their three children.

Contact Machen at (530) 273-8000 or email him at: machen@probrilliance.com.

Chapter One

THOUGHTS ABOUT TIME...

Machen P. MacDonald

When it comes to time management, most experts and coaches will provide what I call the 4 "T"s:

Tricks, Tips, Tools and Tactics

These are all great, necessary, and effective...especially the ones that you choose to actually implement.

However, there is one "T" that doesn't get much thought, at least not conscious thought, and that is Thought itself.

To set the stage, it is important to know that the way we do anything is the way we typically do everything. To understand this, let's direct our thinking to the Manifestation Matrix below. You see, everything begins with a thought. Look around; everything, and I mean everything, began as a seminal thought in someone's mind. Whether it's the light you are reading this book by or the book itself, it started as simply a thought—a form of energy, if you will.

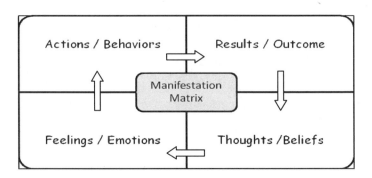

Because we think in images, we tend to evoke emotion in ourselves, or what I call (**e**-motion) or "**e**nergy" in motion. It is this e-motion or feeling that causes us to take either inspired action or *"going through the motion"* action. Perhaps, we take no action at all. It is these actions or behaviors that provide us with our results.

The mistake most people make is assuming that an event triggers an emotion or feeling and that they are hostage to the event or circumstance, rather than a host to their thoughts about the event.

When I am coaching, it is inevitable that the subject of time comes up as a bottleneck for most managers and producers. When I ask questions like, "What is preventing you from getting this project done?" or "What is getting in the way of your success around this goal?," I hear the following *thoughts*:

"There is not enough time…!"
"I don't have time…!"
"I'm running out of time…!"
"I'm swamped!"

"I'm too busy!"
"I'm not good at managing my time…"
"I have other demands on my time…!"
"I have too many demands on my time…!"
"My time is not my own…"
"I don't manage time well…"
"I need to get better at managing my time…"
"I underestimated the time it would take…"

**"What you see depends on what you
thought before you looked."**
- *Eugene Taurman*

Imagine the last time you were up against a quickly approaching deadline. Did you share any of these thoughts? Chances are you did. As you stacked these thoughts on top of one another, notice whether you felt inspired or overwhelmed. What you were feeling was your *thought* energy in motion. Whatever the feeling was when you were thinking these kinds of thoughts, it caused you to behave in a less than resourceful way. Were you making mistakes and being short with the people around you and causing even more consumption of time, or were you in the flow and inspiring to yourself and others and, thereby, leveraging your time?

So, notice what is going on. It is not that these statements are truth or fact. They are simply a thought or a perspective, maybe even a belief that is driving e-motions. They may feel real or factual when you are experiencing the overwhelm of a rapidly approaching deadline. However, it is a bit deeper than that.

It wasn't the event, circumstances, or people involved in the deadline that were causing you anxiety and overwhelm. It was your thoughts about those elements. This is where the work begins. Every one of the great tips, tricks, tools, and tactics you are learning or being reminded about in this book are, for the most part, an action or behavior...a skill set to learn and master. In order to be truly effective with a skill set, you must be the master of your mindset. To become brilliant at mastering your mindset, you must go to the GYM every day.

Going to the G-Y-M

We all know that in order to get your body in shape you need to eat the right foods, avoid or limit the wrong foods, and exercise to strengthen and condition our bodily systems (muscular, cardio, immune, skeletal, respiratory, reproductive, nervous, digestive, endocrine, excretory, integumentary...that's your skin). Okay, maybe you didn't know all of that; however, you knew the eating right and exercising part. The catch is that you need to do this on a regular basis. Once you abandon this regime, it is easy for your body to slip out of peak condition.

In this regard, your mental and emotional conditioning is really no different than your physical conditioning. You must consume the right thoughts and ideas and go to the G-Y-M on a regular basis...You must Guide Your Mind! (G-Y-M) every day. If you are not mentally and emotionally fit, you will not be as resourceful as you can possibly be and, therefore, will not leverage time as effectively.

Reading this book and others like it, attending industry events, self-improvement workshops, being part of mastermind and study groups, and having a coach are all fantastic ways to affect the information and ideas we let into our brains. These elements, which make up part of our memetic environment, otherwise known as the evolution models of cultural informational transfer, are the precursor to our thoughts, beliefs, and ideas of how we see ourselves and the world around us. How we see, based on our thoughts and beliefs, affects how we behave.

One of the greatest minds in the world, Albert Einstein, told us that whatever we say to ourselves before we look at something determines what we see. Our memetic environment has a direct impact on our internal dialogue. If our internal dialogue is running sequences of "There is not enough time…!," "I don't have time for this…!," "I'm running out of time…!," etc., it is no wonder we slip into feelings of overwhelm, anxiety, and an un-resourceful behavior as if we were missing a critical deadline. It's akin to a strangle hold. We can't function accordingly.

We must then learn to control what comes into our mind through our memetic environment, as well as guide our minds on the thoughts that will cause us to feel inspired, focused, and resourceful.

Psychologists and neuro scientists tell us that we typically have over 80,000 thoughts per day. However, 90% of those thoughts are the same thoughts we had yesterday, the day before that, and the day before that, and so on. If it is true that repetition is the mother of skill, then we must be mindful of what we are getting skillful at. Feeling out of control and that there is not enough time is not a good skill to master.

The trick to affecting change is first believing things and people can change, i.e., have the thought or awareness. Then we must align that awareness with action and accountability.

Awareness

Guide Your Mind to the evidence that you have plenty of time. Let's face it. The only moment that truly exists is NOW, and it is never not NOW. The past is gone, and the future does not exist. It's, therefore, always now. If it is always NOW, then you have ALL the time in the world. So, a big part of this game is simply getting and being present with yourself and the situation at hand. Avoid the trap of allowing your thoughts to slip in the past, which typically comes in the forms of regret and judgment. Endeavor to avoid the trap of permitting your thoughts to creep into the future, which typically comes in the form of worry and anxiety. As my friend John Assaraf says, "Worry is just prayer for what you don't want."

Look at the 7 letters ...

N O W H E R E

Did you see No Where or Now Here? Same seven letters and two entirely different meanings. Based upon where you focused, either left of the <u>W</u> or to the right of the <u>W</u>, gave you an entirely different meaning. Here is an analogy: If you are focusing on the left of the W, that is like focusing on the past or future, while focusing on the right of the W is like focusing on the present moment.

With all this being said about being present, there is a definite need for learning from our past and planning for the future. Many people think about what can go wrong or why things won't work. Others with the same level of clarity (they're looking at the same seven letters) see how things can get done and how it will all work out. You see, either way we are making it up because the future has not happened yet.

Based on our focus and what our thoughts are, we create images in our mind. It is these images that either propel us into action or hold us back in fear. So, it is important to maintain the awareness that, regardless of the situation or circumstances we find ourselves in, we always have the power to choose the healthiest perspective. We do that by choosing the right and empowering thoughts. (At the end of this chapter is an assessment, which reveals how you think so you can learn how to maximize your strengths, train and improve your weaknesses, and avoid areas where you are likely to fail.)

Action

Alright, you now have an awareness of how you should be guiding your mind. To affect positive change, you must now combine this awareness with appropriate action.

Here are five things you can do:

1> Guide Your Mind (actually direct your thoughts on what you want to experience)

So, start to adopt thoughts like:

"I get things done on time..."
"There is always enough time..."
"Time exists so I don't have to do it all at once..."
"The only time that is real is now, and it's always now..."
"I am present and, therefore, tapping into my brilliance..."

2> Acknowledge the positive behaviors around how you accomplished things in the time allowed. Avoid finding fault or being critical of yourself. That's not going to serve you. Do this every day so it becomes a habit. I suggest keeping a journal. We know that what we focus on expands. Therefore, if you keep a focus on your positive behaviors, you will perpetuate those and ultimately experience your desired results and outcome.

3> Set the intentions today for what you want to pay attention to and accomplish tomorrow. Doing this will lower your tension. Remember it this way: Set your intention--pay attention—experience low tension. At the end of each day, get clear on what you want to accomplish for the next day. Write it down or input it electronically into whatever system you use for your calendar and task lists. The trick here is to not over commit. I find that many people are playing the over commit game and losing by breaking their commitments to the most important person of all…themselves. This conditions them to actually disregard their commitments and become hostage to whatever things are most recent or have the most emotional content imbedded in them. That's a lousy way to manage ourselves. I suggest that you plan out only 60% of your day. The other 40% will show up just as it is supposed to. Leaders see the invisible so they can achieve the impossible.

4> Success leaves clues. Invest 20 minutes every day in evaluating your effectiveness and the effectiveness of great achievers. Upgrade your memetic environment in the area of time management by reading books, listening to audio, attending workshops, and surfing the websites that pertain to effective self management as it relates to time.

Below is a partial list of some great resources:

- ✓ www.davidco.com
- ✓ www.43folders.com
- ✓ www.franklincovey.com
- ✓ www.salesactivitymanagement.com
- ✓ Getting Things Done by David Allen
- ✓ The One-Minute Organizer by Donna Smallin
- ✓ First Things First by Stephen Covey
- ✓ The 2 Hour House by Brian Conaway and Jose Feliciano
- ✓ The 4-Hour Work Week by Tim Ferris

5> Eliminate, Limit and Delegate:

In your work, become aware of and make a list of these three elements:

A. What you are great at.
B. What you really enjoy doing.
C. What are your five highest revenue-producing activities from those two lists?

The overlap (item C) now becomes your "sweet spot." If you are doing anything that is not on any of those three lists, you are squandering your efforts and energy as time slips by. The strategy here is to eliminate the activities that don't end up on list (A) unless you want to become proficient at it and feel you need to. Just be careful here and make sure it is for your reasons. As for list (B), I suggest acting like a baby. Assuming a baby doesn't like the taste of something, they spit it out right away. When it comes to your time...be a baby. Spit out (eliminate) what you don't like. If the activity you are not good at and don't enjoy is mission critical to your success, then delegate it.

So, the essence here is to stop tolerating, doing, or being what you don't want. If you are to take your business practice and life to the next level, you must stay in your sweet spot as much as possible and eliminate distractions and drains. Delegate what you're not good at to component people who love to do those things. This will avail you of more time so you can expand and increase your sweet spot. Apply this to your personal life, as well. You may not be able to affect this process overnight. Perhaps, that is just a limiting thought ;-). Go for your dreams.

Accountability

The bottom line is it can be a challenge to change our ways relying just on our own will. Regardless of our will power, it only works when we are consciously applying it. Most of us have way too much coming at us throughout the day to stay consciously focused on our key objectives. To help you through this, try enlisting an accountability buddy, get a coach, engage with your spouse or direct report and let them know what you are up to. Let them know of your intentions for the day, week, and month. Request that they check in with you. Try rereading this book and taking five key principles and teaching them to others. Remember to acknowledge and celebrate the WINS! Somewhere between diapers and getting our business cards printed, we stopped celebrating our wins.

By aligning your awareness, action, and accountability, you will become masterful at managing yourself in relation to time sooner rather than later. Enjoy the process of seeing the invisible so you can achieve the impossible.

To take our HVP MindScan and learn more about how you think in the six key dimensions, go to:

www.ProBrilliance.com/client
login: insight
password: success

 **Harry P. Hoopis, CLU, ChFC**, is the Managing Partner of the *Hoopis Financial Group* of Northwestern Mutual in Chicago, IL, and CEO of the *Hoopis Performance Network*. He was inducted into the GAMA International Management Hall of Fame and is the principle author of *The Essentials of Management Development*. You can reach Harry Hoopis at 847-272-3130 or visit him on the web at www.hoopis.com.

Chapter Two

TAKE TIME TO GROW!

Harry P. Hoopis

In my nearly 40 years in business, most of which were spent coaching and encouraging people, I have found that I've had to develop better time control procedures in order to continue growing. Most of what I've learned and taught over the years was discovered out of necessity; and, without it, I would not have experienced growth and success. I learned that as my business evolved through the growth stages from what I refer to as "Small/Small" to "Big/Small" and then from "Small/Big" to "Big/Big," I needed to institute new systems, structure, and routine to keep growing.

First, let's look at some of my personal time control tactics which have emerged over the years. Let's start with one of the worst time management theories I have witnessed, the "open door" policy. What an open door policy really says is, "If you don't have anything to do, stop by and see me, because obviously I don't have anything to do if my door is open and I am susceptible to interruption." Come right in and dump your problem with me; after all, I don't have anything to do. So many years ago, I modified this and said I have an open door policy and the "key" to opening it is an appointment. It seemed like a reasonable request at the time. After all, I have projects, initiatives, and issues to work on, so why not? On the other hand, I want to be there for the coaching and guidance my people have come to expect.

So, I've had to develop simple rules on time management. First of all, a standard appointment for me is 20 minutes in length. For 20 minutes, I'm happy to visit with any of my people and talk about anything they wish. Why did I implement this rule? Truth is, I got tired of people coming in to see me, making small talk for 55 minutes, and then just as I started to look at my watch, concerned about the list of things I still have to do, they would say, "Harry, what I really need to talk about is my wife leaving me, or my kids are in trouble, or my banker is chasing me." Then, we would have to deal with the crisis.

My 20 minute appointments are usually backed up against one another whenever possible to create a "time binder." At 20 minutes, my executive assistant rings three times as an interruption. I can take another two or three minutes to wrap up, and she will call again, if necessary. Now, that might seem a little cold, but here is the second component. When making the appointment, my assistant asks if 20 minutes will be enough. She has permission to offer a longer time slot, if needed. If the person chooses a longer time slot, it has to be accompanied with an agenda. With an agenda, they can have as much time as they like. I have taken an entire day to help some of my associates buy homes, hire staff, purchase cars, or work on their business plans. They know I am there for them, but they need to submit an agenda if they want to spend more than 20 minutes with me.

The next rule to avoid the "drop the crisis on me problem" is that no appointments can be requested for the current day. This accomplishes two things: First, it allows me to look at my day and plan my projects. It allows me to fill my open time slots with specific work. Second, it prevents people from dropping in with what might appear to be a problem before they attempt to solve it themselves. Keep in mind, I do temper this rule. My assistant is instructed that if she senses a major crisis in someone's eyes or voice, she has permission to schedule a five minute meeting as soon as possible. If this occurs, I will walk out of my office and personally assess the situation. We don't sit down until I ask, "What's up?" If I deem it needs my time, then we sit down and deal with it. Sometimes, I might send them off to see or contact a more appropriate person to help them. An important point here is my assistant has the freedom to make this call. I trust her judgment; and if it happens that it really wasn't a crisis, we let it pass.

Here are a few other practical time control measures I picked up over the years. Several times a day, I ask, "What is the best use of my time right now?" This prioritization technique helps me stay focused on the most important things, not just what is urgent. This sometimes results in me having to get out of my office to do some management duties, but if that's the most important, so be it. Next, I try to handle each piece of paper just once. Sometimes, it simply means prioritizing and placing it in its proper file for further attention. My assistant also screens my mail and keeps a "Friday File" for me. The "Friday File" has all the miscellaneous mail in it that she determines I don't need to see until the weekend. Then, I can quickly review it to determine if I need to read it.

Finally, but perhaps the most important of all, Peter Drucker, the renowned management consultant, once said, "Always have the lowest paid person capable of doing the task, do the task." Delegation is the most important time control technique I've ever learned. It not only allows me to focus on the most important aspects of my job, but it's also a key part of my leadership development program. By giving people new tasks, I am able to assess the potential of my key people and give them increasingly more challenging tasks. I call this getting people done through work, as opposed to getting work done through people.

For many years, I have talked about the key to success, particularly among people who are in control of their time. The key to success is to develop systems, structure, and routine for every important thing you do. About 10 years ago, I was speaking to an audience about this topic, and at the end of my presentation, I was approached by a top producer who was in attendance. He said he was intrigued with the concept and wanted to share his daily routine with me. I said, "Go ahead, I am all ears." He went on to tell me he arose at 5:33 a.m. every day. He would go out for his morning run and return home by 6:30. He picked up the paper on the way back into the house and read the newspaper and paperwork from the office while he drank his coffee. At 7:00, his children came down for breakfast, which they enjoyed together. The kids were out the door for school at 7:35, which was when the bus arrived. He would then shower, dress, and arrive at his nearby office by 8:30 a.m. He went on to say that he enjoyed this routine so much that he has carried it over to weekends and even vacations. He told me his life has been enriched by the extra time he has had to read, think, meditate, and plan. He was so excited just talking about it. I was obviously intrigued, but I couldn't help but ask, "Why 5:33 a.m.? Was there some magic in that number?" He smiled and told me when he was setting his digital alarm clock 13 years ago, he accidentally skipped past 5:30 a.m. and didn't want to take the time to go around the digits again! So, it's been 5:33 a.m. for 13 years now! I found all of this amazing, unique, and somewhat inspiring. So, for the last 10 years my alarm has been set for 5:33 a.m.!

Systems, structure, and routine are imperative for people who are in control of their schedules. In talking to other successful people, I have found many who get up at the same time every day and arrive at the office the same time each day. I've seen salespeople who will only eat lunch if they have a new prospect to join them. Imagine the scramble at 11:30 a.m. if one is not booked! You see, the key is that the schedule stays the same day after day and only the people who fill the opening time slots change. Successful salespeople have told me they make their phone calls for appointments the same time each day. As one person said, "I start dialing at 9:00 am, not 9:01!" In addition, I've always recommended quiet time to prepare for your day and buffer or prep time to think carefully about your upcoming day.

Finally, and probably the best of all, is the concept of W.O.R.K™. It's actually "W.O.R.K.ing" in your car. The average person, particularly those in sales, spend an average of three hours in their car every day, moving from home to office and office to appointment. So, for 15 hours per week, you're really serving as you own chauffer! Here is my simple rule. Between the hours of 7:00 a.m. and 7:00

p.m., Monday through Friday, turn off your radio and W.O.R.K. The concept of W.O.R.K. is broken down into two distinct activities. First is the W.O., which stands for "Work Orientation." This is quiet time to think about a variety of things such as your goals, dreams, and aspirations. It can also be spent reflecting on your last appointment, thinking about your next appointment, or rehearsing your sales language in the car. When I started doing this over 35 years ago, people who drove by and saw my lips moving thought I was crazy and was talking to myself! But today, thanks to the invention of the cell phone, they just think I'm on the phone. Think about the benefit of focusing on your vision, your mission, or your family for several hours each week.

The second part of W.O.R.K. is R.K. or "Receive Knowledge." This is your learning time. You should spend this time listening to CD's or I-Pod downloads by other successful people, such as my co-authors, Brian Tracy, Jim Rohn, or Stephen Covey. I can't even tell you how many autobiographies of famous people I've listened to, as well as motivational messages from people in and out of my industry. Now think about this:

3 hours per day x 5 days per week = 15 hours

15 hours per week x 4 weeks per month = 60 hours per month

60 hours per month x 12 months = 720 hours per year

720 hours divided by a typical 40 hour work week = 18 weeks

Imagine 18 weeks of quality time to think, learn, prepare, envision and be inspired.

Practice my W.O.R.K.™ program and grow to a new level!

To access Harry Hoopis' online resources and assessment tools, visit http://www.hoopis.com/pages/resources_assmnt.html

"Time = Life; therefore, waste your time and waste of your life, or master your time and master your life."
- Alan Lakein

Jose Feliciano, CFP, CLU, ChFC, RFC, is CEO of the number one wealth management firm in the national Woodbury Financial Services network, an author, publisher, speaker, industry innovator, and community leader. After 25 years as a wealth management professional, Jose is pioneering new planner training and customer service methods. His thriving firm offers financial planning, employer/ group planning, business advisory, and insurance services. If asked what business he's in, Jose is more likely to say *helping people build their life, legacy, and business—with purpose.* Humble, grateful, energetic and always ready to light the world on fire, Jose was born to deaf-mute parents who moved around a lot. He's been interpreting ever since: first, information for his parents and today, financials for his clients. Jose can be contacted by calling 903-533-8585, sending an email to jose@felicianofinancial.com, or visiting 2hourhouse.com or felicianofinancial.com.

Chapter Three

SEE YOU AT THE TOP!

Jose Feliciano

I'm having the time of my life. My business is thriving, my health is good, my family is happy, and my dreams are realized.

I've realized that how I use time has had a great deal of impact on achieving these milestones. Time could be my enemy or my ally. I chose the latter, and I'd like to share with everyone three experience-based lessons that equipped me with the insights to effectively use time. The lessons: **simplify, delegate, and innovate.** Let me explain.

Simplify

I was the firstborn to two deaf-mute parents. I learned sign language while learning to walk. Soon, there were four more Feliciano siblings, and I was the interpreter for the entire family. It quickly became clear that simplifying a message (for my parents) saved time. I learned that using stories made it easier and faster for people to get meaning. Analogies provided an interpretation shortcut to message clarity without compromising communication quality.

The lesson: Think about the *person* you are communicating with today. Consider their background, their history, and the things that have meaning to them. Then, simplify what you want to communicate to them by using an example, an analogy or story *they* can relate to, and you'll improve the relationship you have with them, while also saving time delivering a message correctly the first time, every time.

Delegate

Twenty-five years ago, I founded Feliciano Financial in Tyler, Texas. Two months ago, my gifted staff and I were honored as the number one advisory firm in the nation (among nearly 2,000 Woodbury Financial advisors). One of the time-related principles that played a role in my success was demonstrating how our busy, high-net worth clients would benefit by delegating their wealth management needs (investments, insurance, company 401K plans, etc.) to our firm so they had more time to do what they do best and love most. I teach the same principle to my staff. We are all blessed with the ability to do something really well – efficiently, and it is often what we love to do the most.

The lesson: Capitalize on what you do efficiently and delegate the rest. Too often, people say they can't delegate because they aren't the CEO. They believe that just because they are not in a leadership position, they have no one to delegate to throughout the day. This isn't true. Your strength is someone else's weakness. Create alliances, partnerships, and collaborative teams who will *share* the load. They can delegate their weaknesses to you; you do the same for them. You will soar through work duties, produce better quality work, enjoy what you do a lot more, and save enormous time having others do what you don't do well.

Innovate

In October, 2005, in Tyler, Texas, 800-plus volunteers led by Brian Conaway achieved the near impossible by building a 2,249 square foot house in less than 3 hours. Dubbed the 2 Hour House™, the greatest outcome wasn't building a house in record time; it was revolutionizing the approach for successfully building anything.

I witnessed this feat and viewed the video of the event. (I encourage you to watch the life-changing, five-minute version of the video at www.2hourhouse.com.) The experience was so profound that I offered to partner with Brian to develop the 2 Hour House business building techniques that are now sweeping across the nation.

We started this endeavor by defining the eight steps in the 2 Hour House process:

Purpose • Power-Up • Partner • Project • Play • Practice • Pursue • Prosper

I'd like to share a story with you about step five and its role in using innovation to save enormous time. When Brian talked to the cement guys who were to pour the foundation of the 2 Hour House and told them they had less than three hours for the entire process, they laughed. It generally takes three days to pour and set cement to code. This is where "play" became important. When we were kids, anything was possible. We were not encumbered with rules, conditions, or policies. Our imagination, the ultimate playground, ruled!

In our 2 Hour House process, we teach CEOs and those they lead to play again. Let the imagination take over. We knew setting the cement the traditional way would get us a foundation in three days. Since this was not acceptable, we had nothing to lose by playing, experimenting with virtually any idea that came to mind. The cement company delivered. They were innovative and invented a new process that produced a code-quality cement foundation for the home that dried in 22 minutes. They salvaged three full days of time. Astounding!

Now, that's just the beginning of this story. This same concrete mixing process was adopted by the Texas Department of Transportation. The impact? They can now make concrete road repairs in three hours instead of three days. This, in turn, impacts how thousands of drivers are inconvenienced. One innovation, born out of a playful mentality to create an inventive, time-saving solution, now impacts both the building and transportation industries. Amazing!

The Lesson: Imagine how much time you and your team could save if you applied the playful attitude that anything is possible. We only need to invent it. You would improve processes at your firm, reduce stress at home, and yield more free hours to achieve greatness in other areas of your life. Don't let this lesson go. If one team of concrete-pouring volunteers in Tyler, Texas, can do one thing to positively impact two industries, imagine what you can do for your industry (in less time) by learning to *play* again.

Time is not the enemy. Our old habits and inability to simplify, delegate, and innovate are the culprits. All are easily overcome. Try on these practices and see what incredible things come into your life. See you at the top!

"There is only one you for all time.
Fearlessly be yourself."
- Anthony Rapp

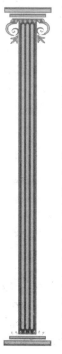

Dr. Stephen R. Covey is the author of several acclaimed books, including the international bestseller, *The 7 Habits of Highly Effective People.* It has sold more than 15 million copies in 38 languages throughout the world. Other bestsellers authored by Dr. Covey include *First Things First, Principle-Centered Leadership* and *The 7 Habits of Highly Effective Families.* Dr. Covey won the 2003 Fatherhood Award from the National Fatherhood Initiative and the Sikh's 1998 International Man of Peace Award. He holds a BS in Business Administration from the University of Utah in Salt Lake City and an MBA in Business Administration from Harvard University. He also has 10 honorary Doctorates. He has made teaching principle-centered living and principle-centered leadership his life's work. To contact Stephen Covey, visit www.franklincovey.com or call 800-819-1812.

Chapter Four

FIRST THINGS FIRST

Stephen R. Covey

I've learned that the good is the enemy of the best when the first things in our lives are subordinated to other things. My daughter, Maria, recently had a new baby. A few days after she delivered, I visited with her, expecting to find her happy. Instead, I found her frustrated. She told me, "I have so many other projects and interests that are important to me. But right now, I have to put everything on hold. I'm spending all my time just meeting the physical needs of this new baby. I can't even find time to be with my other two children and my husband."

Seeking to understand, I replied, "So, this new baby is consuming you?" She continued, "I have other work to do. I have some writing projects that need my attention. I have other people in my life." I asked, "What does your conscience tell you to do? Maybe right now there is only one thing that matters—your baby." She said, "But I have so many other projects and plans." She showed me her organizer. "I schedule time to do these other things, but then I'm constantly interrupted by my baby." I talked to her about the concept of a compass, not a clock. "You're being governed by your internal compass, your conscience, and you're doing something of enormous good. Now is not the time to be controlled by the clock. Throw away your planner for a few weeks. Only one thing is needful. So, relax and enjoy the very nature of this interruption to your life."

"But what about life balance and sharpening the saw?" she asked, knowing I teach these principles. "Your life is going to be imbalanced for a time, and it should be. The long run is where you go for balance. For now, don't even try to keep a schedule. Forget your calendar; take care of yourself; don't worry. Just enjoy the baby, and let that infant feel your joy." I reminded her, "The good is often the enemy of the best. You won't get much satisfaction from fulfilling scheduled commitments if you have to sacrifice first things and best things. Your satisfactions are tied to your role expectations. Maybe the only role that matters this entire day will be mothering your new baby. And if you fulfill that role well, you will feel satisfied. But if you schedule other commitments when you have no control of the demands your baby is going to make, you'll only be frustrated." Maria has since learned to relax and enjoy her baby more. She has also involved her husband and other children more in caring for the new baby, sharing with them all that can be shared.

Identify Your First Things

What are the first things in your life? One good way to answer that question is by asking other questions: "What is unique about me? What are my unique gifts? What is it that I can do that no one else can do?" For instance, who else can be a father to your child? A grandparent to your grandchildren? Who else can teach your students? Who else can lead your company? Who else can be a mother to your baby? In a sense, we all have our "babies," meaning some demanding new project or product.

Each of us has unique talents and capabilities and important work to do in life. The tragedy is that our unique contribution is often never made because the important "first things" in our lives are choked out by other urgent things. So, some important works are never started or finished. In our new book, *First Things First*, co-authored with Roger and Rebecca Merrill, we suggest that the path to personal leadership follows the stepping stones of vision, mission, balance, roles, goals, perspective, and integrity in the moment of choice. It's an ecological balancing process. We invite readers to think very carefully through this process. "What are my responsibilities in life? Who are the people I care about?" The answers become the basis for thinking through your roles.

Your goals are then set by asking, "What is the important future state for each relationship or responsibility?" Setting up win-win agreements with people and maintaining positive relationships is not an efficient process; in fact, the process is usually slow. But once a win-win agreement is in place, the work will go fast. If you're efficient up front, you might be taking the slowest approach. Yes, you might drum your decision down someone else's throat, but whether or not he is committed to live by that decision and to carry it out is a different matter. Slow is fast; fast is slow. Peter Drucker makes the distinction between a quality decision and an effective decision. You can make a quality decision; but if there isn't commitment to it, it won't be effective. There has to be commitment to make a "quality decision" effective. An executive may be highly efficient working with things, but highly ineffective working with people. Efficiency is different in kind from effectiveness. Effectiveness is a results word; efficiency is a methods word. Some people can climb the "ladder of success" very efficiently, but if it's leaning against the wrong wall, they won't be effective.

Efficiency is the value you learn when you work with things. You can move things around fast: you can move money, manage resources, and rearrange your furniture quickly. But if you try to be efficient with people on jugular issues, you'll likely be ineffective. You can't deal with people as if you're dealing with things. You can be efficient with things, but you need to be effective with people, particularly on jugular issues. Have you ever tried to be efficient with your spouse on a tough issue? How did it go? If you go fast, you'll make very slow progress. If you go slow and get deep involvement doing what is necessary through synergistic communication based on a win-win spirit, you'll find that in the long run it's fast because then you have total commitment to it. You also have a quality decision simply because you have the benefit of different creative ideas interacting, creating a new solution that is better and more bonding.

Subordinate Clock to Compass

For many executives, the dominant metaphor of life is still the clock. We value the clock for its speed and efficiency. The clock has its place, efficiency has its place—after effectiveness. The symbol of effectiveness is the compass— a sense of direction, purpose, vision, perspective, and balance. A well-educated conscience serves as an internal monitoring and guidance system. To move from a clock to a compass mindset, you focus on moving the fulcrum over by empowering other people. But the empowerment process itself is not efficient. You can't think control; you think of releasing feelings seldom expressed and interacting with others until you create something better. You don't know what it is at the beginning. It takes a lot of internal security, a lot of self-mastery, before you can even assume that risk. And the people who like to control their time, money, and things tend to try to control people, taking the efficiency approach, which in the long run is very ineffective. Effectiveness applies to self as much as to other people. You should never be efficient with yourself, either.

For example, one morning I met with a group in our training program. Someone said, "Creating a personal mission statement is a tough process." I said, "Well, are you approaching it through an efficiency paradigm or an effectiveness paradigm? If you use the efficiency approach, you may try to bang it out this weekend. But if you use the effectiveness approach, you'll carry on this tortuous internal debate on every aspect of your nature, your memory system, your imagination system, your value system, your old habits, old scripts. You'll keep this dialogue going until you feel at peace." Why do executives find it easy to schedule and keep appointments with others, but hard to keep appointments with themselves? If people can make and keep promises to themselves, they will significantly increase their social integrity. Conversely, if they learn to make and keep promises to others, they will have higher self-discipline. The private victory of keeping appointments with ourselves doesn't just mean that we spend some private time alone; it might also mean that we promise ourselves not to overreact or to apologize in the middle of a mistake. Keeping these promises enormously increases our sense of integrity.

For example, the other day, I saw my son chew out his little sister for rearranging his office. He had everything laid out to work on his project, but she thought it was messy and she wanted to help her brother. In the middle of his tirade, he caught himself and said, "I apologize. I'm just taking my frustrations out on you, and I know you meant to do well." He did it right then. He kept an appointment with himself to live by his values even in the heat of the moment. I admired him enormously. Knowing that people and relationships are more important than schedules and things, we can subordinate a schedule without feeling guilty because we superordinate the conscience, the commitment to a larger vision and set of values. We subordinate the clock approach of efficiency to the compass approach of effectiveness. When using the compass, we subordinate our schedules to people, purposes, and principles. The "mega priorities" of the compass subordinate the "mini priorities" of the clock. When your projects are worthy ones, then your purpose will transcend petty concerns and matters of secondary importance.

What Charles Dickens learned from writing *A Christmas Carol* is that a transcendent purpose subordinates the old scripts of scarcity and independence. It may not totally erase them, but at least it subordinates them. Dickens got a strong sense of purpose about writing a story that would bless the lives of families, particularly children, when he reflected on the time when he worked in the factories 12 hours a day, every day of the week, and his father and other members of his family were in debtor's prison for several months. He remembered those times of scarcity and recognized them as scripts. As he combined the images of the present with the past, he experienced an enormous burst of creative energy that subordinated all of his present problems, his depression, and the possibility of financial ruin to get out this magnificent story.

Without valuing interdependence and abundance thinking, you won't be able to keep first things first. Some people never understand these realities. They fall back into independence and scarcity thinking. Those perspectives are more a function of scripting than of anything else. But, we can change the script.

From Urgency to Importance

When we are guided by an internal compass, a highly educated conscience, we may decide to dedicate an entire morning to one person or to focus on one project and subordinate an earlier schedule we'd set up (unless we have strong commitments to meet with certain individuals, then we work around those). Or, we may decide to set aside an afternoon to keep an appointment only with ourselves. During that time, we might sharpen the saw by exercising one or more of the four dimensions of our personality: physical, mental, social, and spiritual. We use self-awareness to know what to do and when.

I recommend a time management credo that says: "I will not be governed by the efficiency of the clock; I will be governed by my conscience, because my conscience deals with the totality of my life. Since it is well educated from study and from experience, it will help me make wise decisions." Under the influence of a well-developed conscience, you make decisions on a daily, hourly, and moment-to-moment basis to be governed by principles. If you are immersed in extremely productive or creative work, don't let anything interrupt. Can you imagine a surgeon taking a telephone call in the middle of surgery? Most people are buried in urgency. Most production and management jobs call for quick reactions to what is urgent and important. The net effect of a reactionary, urgent lifestyle is stress, burnout, crisis management, and always putting out fires. If you're into daily planning and prioritizing, then, by definition, you live with urgencies and crises. Important, but not urgent, activities are easily pushed out by daily planning. When you are guided by an internal compass or set of principles, you begin to see that the idea that I am in control is an arrogant concept. You have to humbly submit yourself to natural laws that ultimately govern, anyway. If you internalize those laws and principles, you create a highly educated conscience. And if you are open to it, you will keep first things first.

Scott Taylor is the Founder and CEO of TaylorMade Marketing, LLC, a Los Angeles based creative agency formed in 1996 and focused on search engine optimization, copy and design for business collateral materials, creation and maintenance of ecommerce web sites, and promotional campaigns online and in print. Scott is also the President and Head Coach of FastPath Coaching (a TaylorMade Marketing Company) providing FastPath action plans to small business owners and sales professionals via coaching, seminars, and workshops year round. In February, 2008 Scott formally accepted the position of being an Executive Coach, Facilitator, and Chair with Vistage International (formerly TEC), the World's Leading Chief Executive Organization (www.vistage.com). Scott Taylor can be reached at FastPath Coaching by calling 818-344-6800, sending an email to scott@fastpathcoaching.com or visiting www.fastpathcoaching.com.

Chapter Five

"TIME"
(IMAGINE · CREATE · DELIVER)

Scott Taylor

"Ticking away the moments that make up a dull day
You fritter and waste the hours in an offhand way
Kicking around on a piece of ground in your home town
Waiting for someone or something to show you the way."

Pink Floyd "Time"
(Dark Side of the Moon) Circa. 1973

The very second Machen MacDonald asked me to contribute to this book on time management, I had the idea of using the Pink Floyd lyrics from "Time" throughout my article to support my points!

A strong 48 years of influence by a fantastic mom, older brothers and sisters, as well as 43-plus years of brilliant teachers, leaders, managers, and mentors all stressed to me at times how fleeting our time is here in this life, which may be why the words of the Pink Floyd song "Time" have always been with me since the release of that album.

I always thought that Roger Waters and David Gilmour just nailed the point that no other manager or teacher ever really added much to for me! I was just 13 years old when Dark Side of the Moon was released, and my best friend, Jeff Herman, and I were so impressed. We had already decided to start our rock band and help change the world with music and messages, like our musical mentors were doing for us! This album was a life changer for many of us! We thought we were so deep and connected. Maybe we were, but that was then, and if I have anything to add of merit and grace… it's that all we really have is now! Time matters in this physical-time based reality.

All that really matters in terms of encouraging our teams, ourselves, as well as the next generations to any measurable degree, is to consider what we will do with each "now!"

I thought I knew it all so perfectly then, but I really didn't have the depth that perhaps only age (or "Time" itself) provides.

> *"Tired of lying in the sunshine*
> *Staying home to watch the rain*
> *And you are young and life is long*
> *And there is time to kill today*
> *And then one day you find*
> *Ten years have got behind you*
> *No one told you when to run*
> *You missed the starting gun"*

Pink Floyd "Time" (2nd verse)
(Dark Side of the Moon) Circa. 1973

If only we really could have known that all those thoughts, all those ideas, all those desires, and all those wants and wishes were "starting guns" that we just ignored or creatively put on the eternal back burner and may be gone now forever... or, maybe not!

I believe to my core that each powerful idea of positive desire that pulls us and begs us into action are things we could have attained, in fact, would have attained had we only made the move and sustained long enough. If we thought it with any real intent, we had the potential, the capacity, contacts, creativity, and the power to succeed. This is not about regret for what could have been. It's more important to simply acknowledge the lesson or risk making the same mistakes redundantly until we do.

Obviously, the options still exist if the desire is still present, so I'm not engaging the regret stage. Yet, I hope you will take away this--that if it was true then, it is just as true now! Time hasn't changed; we have! Remember our best asset for tomorrow is today! Our only hope for what's next is "NOW!"

The lessons of yesterday are less about the knowledge we gain; the lessons are only truly useful if we take better action when we are faced with the next test. Will you follow your bliss, or will you miss the starting gun again?

Tomorrow is counting on today! I love this line of thinking because it's a lot like the mystery that unfolds as we discover deeper thinkers who challenge our beliefs--just like the Pink Floyd album opened doors of deeper thought for me and Jeff. We were very impressed with the deeper lyric of the Pink Floyd songs, which may have been composed under the influence of psychedelic chemical alteration (no doubt), but we just liked what we heard. It beat the hell out of anything we were hearing on the radio at the time. It actually made us think about our time and purpose here, and we were only here for 13 years at the time!

If you will create anything you want, you will need to harness and co-create with nature, with whatever you are aware enough to see and engage with. For me, I have a strong sense that it is time to mentor, to coach all who will listen (or read). What is it for you?

What will you do with your time? We all have so much potential, but potential is meaningless unless we act on our thoughts, and we must be the artists and sculpt our thoughts, beliefs, and habits until they begin to serve our true desires, wants, and wishes! Seek out the answers as you have with this book. Never stop your search until you are truly satisfied, then, uplevel your goals again. That is our true nature!

The point is that we have enough time! Time is not the issue if we will make engaging and getting into action a more established habit! A thought is not, and never will be, enough. The knowledge we gain will never really be enough. The contacts we make will never really be enough to serve the full scope, and any component of what "it" takes by itself is just simply not enough to make a worthy thing happen. It's a co-creation.

We also have to be wise to the fact that action without the knowledge, the plan, the contacts, and any or all of the other factors and concerns would also be foolish on its own. Again, it's a co-creation. The best stuff happens with co-creation! To take a note from Einstein, who wrote that "nothing happens until something moves," it may be hard for most to accept that we are what needs to move first! It might serve some better to say that none of your dreams will happen until you make them happen!

> *"And you run, and you run to catch up with the sun,*
> *but it's sinking*
> *Racing around to come up behind you again*
> *The sun is the same in a relative way, but you're older*
> *Shorter of breath and one day closer to death"*

Pink Floyd "Time" (3rd verse)
(Dark Side of the Moon) Circa. 1973

One of the most powerful ideas for creating an emotionally compelling outcome was shared with me recently, and I would like to share it with you. This is another good example of allowing co-creation. I will suggest an exercise that should take between five and fifteen minutes to complete, depending on how deep you would like to go with it.

Imagine that you just received a fantastic testimonial from one of the most important, impressive, and influential people you could ever imagine! Do that now. Make it real in your mind. Once the feelings begin to bubble up, you'll know that you are on track to doing this properly!

I want you to imagine this is actually happening, it's real. It's more than you ever imagined because you know how much effort you put out, and this time, you must have really put your heart into your work, and you made an outstanding impact and the results are just amazing! YOU DID IT! Use your mind now... Imagine that you did it, you deserve it, you changed lives this time, and you just received the ultimate testimonial...What will it say? How will you feel?

Now hold on to these emotions, and go for it. Create it now so that you can hold it in your hands. Begin writing down whatever you might wish to see on the ultimate testimonial of your dreams. Write out as "in a perfect world" exactly what you wish would be written on this amazing testimonial.

What did they write? It's your dream; it can be anything you really want! Write the testimonial you would most like to receive, and you will be giving yourself a gift that can literally change your life!

I hope you will be playful enough to engage with this important exercise. Do this with your team and watch their faces light up. That's what happened for me. We tend to get out of life what we put into it, so really go for it and enjoy the results. Then keep it and intend to make it happen. Having this testimonial provides some clarity that just isn't found any other way. We create our future anyway, so why not use your imagination more creatively and see what bubbles up for you!

Einstein also taught us that "imagination is more important than knowledge." This exercise is catalyst to that point! All of our problems are in our imagination, and so are our ultimate solutions! Reconnect with a powerful intention. Imagine that you can, and you can! You can do what you want, and you can have what you want, but you will have to listen for the "starting gun." Maybe that's an idea that you have not completed or have been putting off. I believe it's a great habit to nurture!

Winners act on their ideas more habitually! Winners also tend to finish or follow through more often, and that's what it takes to be a winner in life! To repeat an earlier point: All that really matters in terms of encouraging our teams, ourselves, as well as the next generations to any measurable degree, is to consider what we will do with each "now!"

"Every year is getting shorter
Never seem to find the time
Plans that either come to nought
Or half a page of scribbled lines
Hanging on in quiet desperation is the English way
The time is gone, The song is over
Thought I'd something more to say"

Pink Floyd "Time" (4th verse)
(Dark Side of the Moon) Circa. 1973

Will you act on it? Will you act on the idea that you've had more than once or the next powerful concept that pulls you and somehow you just know it could work if you give it more attention and time? One of my mentors likes to remind me often that I will live with discipline or regret! Discipline is very light compared to the heavy emotional pain of regret!

We teach our staff, our students, and our children by our actions, not just our words. What are you teaching yours?

Another great line of thinking is, "What we can do is often worlds away from what we will do;" yet, what we will do is most connected to the life we get to live, experience, and share with those we love and influence the most.

Often, it is more helpful to put ourselves into an environment that increases the likelihood of peak performing! Some environments will empower us, while other environments weaken our will or even take us down to levels of depression.

Get on purpose; get clear on what motivates you into action. Start a list of what that might be for you. For most people, it's about being around positive, forward-thinking "Can-Do" people and putting your intentions out there as goals and objectives so that others of influence will be an accountability partner for you more often. The time you spend with positive people will impact your life more than anything else! This can save you a lot of wasted time.

This is why an undisciplined young man in the army for two days is changed forever! Suddenly, on day one his bed is made, his shoes are shined, and his clothes are folded and ready for inspection by anyone on earth! He is stronger willed, open to positive suggestions, ready to serve, and will listen more attentively than ever before in his young life! This is an extreme environment which demands peak performance.

Likewise, when my students show up for my FastPath sales and marketing boot camps, I enjoy the attitudes they bring. They are ready to apply what they learn with an open mind and acknowledge the discipline required to make the necessary change to live the life they want and wish for! The ones who "hear the starting gun" and get into action in those first weeks are changed forever, and those who put it off never seem to find the time!

Time is a master's tool! Schedule everything that is important to you and your goals. Most people won't schedule anything, and that is why most people are poor, bored, and living a desperate life full of fear, doubt, and anxiety. Use your time wisely, and you will not only reach more of your goals, you will be much happier, and you will inspire others.

Home, home again
I like to be here when I can
When I come home cold and tired
It's good to warm my bones beside the fire
Far away across the field
The tolling of the iron bell
Calls the faithful to their knees
To hear the softly spoken magic spells
(Tic toc, tic toc, tic toc...)

Pink Floyd "Time" (5th verse)
(Dark Side of the Moon) Circa. 1973

So then, what will you do with this information? The big question of our life is, "What will we "do" with our time here?" There are a million quotes on time, and it's a safe bet that my co-authors have done a good job at sharing most of the great ones with you. Seek them out. Go and write them down. What could be more inspirational?

This book in your hands right now can absolutely change your life! It only asks for your co-creation in doing so!

Imagine, Create, and Deliver whatever you want in this life using the time you are given! The starting gun may not always be something you will hear. It may be a feeling or hunch, or it may be triggered by someone or something else! Trust that you will know and move in the direction of your dreams!

Seek clarity so that you will know what to measure. Get into action so that your time is not squandered away. You only have so much to work with.

Engage with others to deliver what they really want, and they will be just as inspired to help you.

When we get this right, we "get to" do the work of our desires, wants, and wishes, and never again be forced or "have to" do something just to pay the bills!

Time will be very good to you when you use each day with respect for time and maintain a healthy, open "can do" mindset. Live your life full-out, going for it with the intention and carefree excitement you were born with as a baby!

How will you consider your lessons from your past?

How will you act on your dreams?

How will you allow others to play a role in co-creation?

How will you use your NOW?

It's all now!

Imagine, Create, Deliver.

Enjoy!

"Until you value yourself, you will not value your time. Until you value your time, you will not do anything with it."
- M. Scott Peck

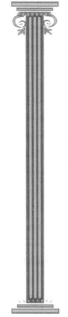 **Ruben Gonzalez** is a three-time Olympian and the author of *The Courage to Succeed,* which is endorsed by business experts Ken Blanchard, Stephen Covey, and Brian Tracy. Ruben has appeared nationally on ABC, CBS, and NBC and been featured in Time Magazine, BusinessWeek, and Success Magazine. Recently, he co-starred in the motivational movie *Pass It On!* Ruben is the founder of TheOlympicSpeaker.com, a firm dedicated to inspiring and equipping people to achieve their goals. Ruben speaks to organizations around the world about leadership, team building, mastering change and overcoming obstacles on the way to the top.

To contact Ruben Gonzalez, telephone (832) 689-8282 or visit www.TheOlympicSpeaker.com.

Chapter Six

HOW TO HIT YOUR GOALS
IN HALF THE TIME

Ruben Gonzalez

Would you like to be able to reach your goals in half the time? Would you like to be able to work on many projects effectively?

If I could do it, you can, too. I'm a three-time Olympian in the sport of luge. Thanks to consistently following some simple time management tips, I've been able to successfully work on several big projects simultaneously for many years.

I used to think that you could only work on one project at a time. Then, about 20 years ago, I read "The Art of the Deal" by Donald Trump. The best part in Trump's book is the section called "A Week in the Life." It's a log of a week's worth of Trump's meetings and phone calls.

I was amazed to discover that Trump is working on 10 to 12 major deals at any one time. I didn't think that was possible until I learned the principles of time management.

Today, thanks to mastering the time management principles you are learning in this book, I have no problem building my business, TheOlympicSpeaker.com, writing books, creating learning programs, traveling the world speaking for companies and organizations, and training for my fourth Winter Olympics. I still find plenty of time to be active in my church, do charity work, mentor other speakers, and spend quality and quantity time with my family. In fact, in addition to several family vacations every year, I get to take my daughter on six to eight weekend camping trips a year.

I'm just an ordinary guy, and the principles work for me. If they work for me, they will work for you…

The first step in time management is to make a list of the tasks you'll need to complete in order to achieve each of your goals and to prioritize your list. The second step in managing your time is to start planning your weeks and your days in advance. Sunday evening is a great time to plan your week, and the end of your workday is a great time to plan your next day. Remember…plans change, but the act of planning gets you to think about the road ahead and saves you time in the long run.

Why plan the night before? Because if you do, your subconscious mind will work on your task list all night long. Often, you'll wake up in the morning with ideas and insights that will help you during the day.

Prioritize your task list. Determine which tasks are urgent and which are truly important. Most people spend their days working on urgent tasks that are not important. People who are constantly reacting to outside pressures

(pressures like answering the phone, interruptions, putting out fires, etc.) are stressed and out of control.

The most effective people focus on important tasks and put the urgent tasks on the back burner. Important tasks are those that will have the biggest impact on your long-term goals. Focus on those.

Prioritizing your tasks is critical because whenever you work on a particular task, you are choosing not to work on all of the other tasks. That is why your choice of which tasks you work on will determine your future. Do you want to leave your future to chance, or is your future worth planning for?

Once you start working on a task, work on it until it is completed. Focus on only one task at a time. Thomas Edison, arguably the greatest inventor in American history, said that his success was due to his ability to work continuously on one task until he was finished. If it's good enough for Edison, don't you think it's good enough for you and me?

Plan your day in a way that it will give you long, uninterrupted chunks of work time—60 to 90 minute chunks of time. When your mind is focused on a single task for long periods of time, you will accomplish many times more work than if you are working on several tasks simultaneously.

Finally, learn to say "NO" to anything that will keep you from achieving your goals. Focus single-mindedly on your desired end result, and you will be amazed at how much you achieve in your life.

To receive a complimentary copy of Ruben's <u>new</u> book,
"Becoming Unstoppable," go to
www. TheOlympicSpeaker.com

"To achieve great things, two things are
needed; a plan, and not quite enough time."
- Leonard Bernstein

This is the beginning of a new day.

God has given me this day to use as I will.

I can waste it or use it for good.

What I do today is important, because

I am exchanging a day of my life for it.

When tomorrow comes,

This day will be gone forever,

Leaving in its place something

That I have traded for it.

I want it to be gain, not loss;

Good not evil; success not failure;

In order that I shall not regret

The price I paid for it.

--Author Unknown

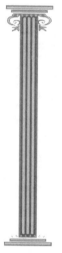

Alison Arnold Ph.D., "Doc Ali," is internationally known as a liberator of fear and greatness. She works extensively with Olympic athletes, corporate executives, and individuals committed to living extraordinary lives. She can be seen on VH1 in "Scott Baio is 45 and...Single." For more information on Doc Ali and to sign her mailing list for informational newsletters and events, please go to www.screamandrunnaked.com.

You can reach Doc Ali at 602-495-9300 or by email: to docalison@aol.com

Chapter Seven

CONSCIOUS TIME MANAGEMENT: INCREDIBLE PRODUCTIVITY IN THE INCREDIBLE PRESENT

Alison Arnold, Ph.D.

It is the most precious thing there is. More precious than money, it is the one thing that you never get more of or get back. No matter how rich, successful, or famous one is, it continues to deplete with every second of the ticking clock. In my work with successful business executives and Olympic athletes, I hear this complaint over and over again, "I just don't have enough time." So, how can you slow it down? How can you create a day so purposeful and on task that it feels as if you effortlessly get everything done?

The key to effortless productivity is as simple as breathing in and out. It's a secret I learned during a four-month stay in a mountain monastery in Nepal. I went to Nepal because I didn't feel fully alive. I felt similar to a cog in a machine. I was running from appointment to appointment. My day timer was filled with meetings, and I seemed to get little done. I was forgetting critical details about the lives of my clients, not to mention my loved ones. I woke up every morning dreading the fullness of the day and went to sleep at night with anxiety about what didn't get done, not to

69

mention what needed to be done tomorrow. I had so much to do and so little time. I could never be enough or have enough. Did these monks in Nepal have some secrets to share with me? Did they even understand my culture or what I was going through? The monks shared a way of conscious time management beginning the moment one wakes up to the moment one goes to sleep that has changed not only how much I accomplish in a day, but the manner in which I go about getting it done.

Step One: Begin Your Day with Optimism

Instead of starting your day with the anxiety of all you need to get done, begin with a statement of positivity and optimism. Statements like, "I know my day will evolve exactly as it needs to," and "I'm excited to see what happens today," facilitate a mental state of flow rather than a state of force. Psychologist Mihaly Csikszenmihalyi compares the state of flow to what sport psychologists call being "in the zone." This is a state of positive, transcendent absorption in which you stretch beyond your limits and anything feels possible. In a state of flow, you feel alert, unselfconscious, and totally absorbed in the present moment. This is the realm of productivity.

We can all identify with days when the first thought upon waking is, "How am I ever going to make it through this day?" We hide under the covers hoping some miracle occurs leading to a surprise day off. Beginning your day with anxiety leads to forcing, and whether you are out on the playing field or in the boardroom, forcing is never the energy of success. Always begin your day in a state of joy and excitement rather than stress, worry, and negativity.

Use rituals of breathing, positive self-talk, enjoying your morning coffee, or reading something inspirational to put yourself in a mental state conducive to achieving your best results.

Conscious Time Action: When you wake up tomorrow morning, make your first thought a positive statement about your day. Before you get out of bed, set the mood of optimism about what you will accomplish.

Step Two: Set Clear Intentions for Your Day

In every moment, you make a choice. Every moment is filled with intention. And every moment these choices and intentions create your life and your day. Intention is like a directional laser beam for your mind, and thus your life. When your mind is scattered on many tasks, ideas, and projects, your laser is diffused, having little power. Intention requires focus. Have you ever tried to ignite paper or a piece of wood using a magnifying glass? If you keep moving the glass from place to place, even the magnified power of the sun's beams through the lens will not start a fire. But if you hold the magnifying lens perfectly still, you can harness the power of the sun by focusing the rays in a concentrated beam of energy, and you will ignite a fire. Specific intention aligns the power of your thoughts to one strong, direct current of energy. Laser-like intention is where all the action happens. It's where decisions are made and projects completed.

Decide what you want to do each day. Commit to it. Take five minutes, make a list and write your intentions down as early in the day as possible. Ask yourself, "What do I want to accomplish today?" The answer to this question can range from "nothing" to any number of tasks on your daily list. Make it a part of your morning ritual, or write them down first thing upon arriving to work. If your days drift by without setting definite intentions for what you want to accomplish, your day becomes directionless, without much structure or purpose. Set clear intentions for the tasks on your plate each day.

Conscious Time Action: *Either during your morning routine or first thing upon your arrival at the office, write your intentions of what you want to accomplish today. Be specific and realistic in your goals.*

Step Three: Your Power is in the Present

Your mind can only focus on one thing at a time. As much as you may think multi-tasking saves time, it is actually shaving off precious minutes of your day, not to mention compromising the quality of your task or interaction. There is nothing less productive than thinking about many projects, tasks, and conversations while focusing on none. Thich Nhat Hanh, a Buddhist monk, says that everything we do can be an act of poetry (not to mention productivity) if we are fully present. The Sutra of Mindfulness reads,

> *"When walking, the practitioner must be conscious that he is walking. When sitting, the practitioner must be conscious that he is sitting. When lying down, the practitioner must be conscious that he is lying down."*

So, if we take the Sutra to heart, when e-mailing, we are conscious of e-mailing. When working on next year's budget, we are conscious of next year's budget. When talking to a manager, we are conscious of talking to that manager. Worrying about the future, perseverating over the past, and getting involved in the drama of others are all distractions pulling you out of the present. How often do your thoughts wander away from what you are doing?

The Buddha called the mind "a monkey" or a "wild horse." The monkey-mind sets up a constant internal chatter, calculating and scheming, quarreling and debating, remembering wrongs against "me and mine." The monkey-mind loves to run away from tasks into daydreams, to wander far without warning into the past or future, and to return when it pleases. Bring your mind back from distracting mental "field trips" by focusing on your breathing or using a key word or phrase. Many times, saying something to yourself like "back to task" can reel in the crazy antics of the monkey-mind and get it back on track. Set a specific amount of time to devote one-pointed attention to a task. Then do it. Avoid wasting precious time and keep your mind on the task at hand until completed or you intentionally take a needed break.

Conscious Time Action: *Be aware of when your monkey- mind is on and off task. If your mind wanders, bring it back to task by simply focusing on your breathing and saying "back on task" for as many minutes as you have left in this work cycle.*

Step Four: Take Conscious Breaks

One can't stay in peak performance mode 100% of the time. Even the elite athlete needs recovery to perform at the highest levels. During your day take conscious breaks.

Don't simply numb your mind for an hour, surfing the internet or being drained by the office gossip. Choose consciously to take a certain amount of time, relaxing your mind and body from stress. Go for a walk outside, talk to an inspiring co-worker, eat your lunch mindfully. Again, set a specific amount of time for mental recovery, but be sure to give your body and mind what it needs to recharge your battery back to full.

Conscious Time Action: *Plan breaks during the day to refuel your mind and body. Remember, a short break when you need one can save you hours of wasted nonproductive time.*

Step Five: End Your Day in Gratitude

The end of the day is a time for assessment and gratitude. Place your attention on achievements. Most people can list all that did not get done, but have trouble acknowledging their accomplishments. At the end of your work day, notice everything you accomplished and express gratitude for the things that went well. Take the time to write them down, along with your list of projects for the next day. Evaluate what did not get accomplished in a non-judgmental manner, write them on the list for tomorrow, and let it go. Don't beat yourself up for deeds not done. Both worry and self-criticism are time wasters. Be prepared with statements that help you stay calm and relaxed. Statements like, "I did all I could do" and "The world will not end if it's done tomorrow" will help build compassion for self and others. There is so much to be grateful for every day—the people in your life, the friends who brought you joy, and the ones who taught you painful lessons. Celebrate it all.

Conscious Time Action: *At the end of your workday or before bed, notice and write three things you are grateful for that occurred during that day. Take special notice of your joys and accomplishments.*

As I sat at my mountain monastery in Nepal, my teachers would often quote the Buddha, "If anything is worth doing," they would say, "do it with all your heart." This two-part statement is important to consider when looking at your time management practice. The first part, "If anything is worth doing," is a call to contemplation. Why are you doing this task? Search for the reasons and purpose for your actions. Every action should be in line with your greater purpose and goals in some capacity. It is very appropriate to consistently ask yourself the simple question, "Is this task worth doing?" If the answer is yes, then the second part of the Buddha's quote is applicable. Whether it be planning a project, listening to voicemails, or responding to an agitated client, do it with all your heart. A life fully lived is a life without holding back. Do every task as if it were the most important task of your life. Enjoy each one thoroughly, noticing its individual beauty and purpose. When you can find the beauty in the mundane, you really begin to see the world as the extraordinary place that it is.

Even with all these practices, there is no guarantee you will get everything done on your plate of the impossible. But as long as you follow the method of the Nepalese monks, two things are certain, your productivity will have the power of the present, and you'll be a much happier person along the way.

Jim Rohn is America's Foremost Business Philosopher.

To subscribe to the Free Jim Rohn Weekly E-Zine, visit www.jimrohn.com or send a blank email to Subscribe@jimrohn.com.

Chapter Eight

ENDING PROCRASTINATION

Jim Rohn

Perseverance is about as important to achievement as gasoline is to driving a car. Sure, there will be times when you feel like you're spinning your wheels, but you'll always get out of the rut with genuine perseverance. Without it, you won't even be able to start your engine.

The opposite of perseverance is procrastination. Perseverance means you never quit. Procrastination usually means you never get started, although the inability to finish something is also a form of procrastination.

Ask people why they procrastinate and you'll often hear something like, "I'm a perfectionist. Everything has to be just right before I can get down to work. No distractions, not too much noise, no telephone calls interrupting me, and, of course, I have to be feeling well physically, too. I can't work when I have a headache."

The other end of procrastination—being unable to finish— also has a perfectionist explanation: "I'm just never satisfied. I'm my own harshest critic. If all the i's aren't dotted and all the t's aren't crossed, I just can't consider

77

that I'm done. That's just the way I am, and I'll probably never change."

Do you see what's going on here? A fault is being turned into a virtue. The perfectionist is saying that his standards are just too high for this world. This fault-into-virtue syndrome is a common defense when people are called upon to discuss their weaknesses, but, in the end, it's just a very pious kind of excuse making. It certainly doesn't have anything to do with what's really behind procrastination.

Remember, the basis of procrastination could be fear of failure. That's what perfectionism really is, once you take a hard look at it. What's the difference whether you're afraid of being less than perfect or afraid of anything else? You're still paralyzed by fear. What's the difference whether you never start or never finish? You're still stuck. You're still going nowhere. You're still overwhelmed by whatever task is before you. You're still allowing yourself to be dominated by a negative vision of the future in which you see yourself being criticized, laughed at, punished, or ridden out of town on a rail. Of course, this negative vision of the future is really a mechanism that allows you to do nothing. It's a very convenient mental tool.

I'm going to tell you how to overcome procrastination. I'm going to show you how to turn procrastination into perseverance, and if you do what I suggest, the process will be virtually painless. It involves using two very powerful principles that foster productivity and perseverance instead of passivity and procrastination.

The first principle is: Break it down.

No matter what you're trying to accomplish, whether it's writing a book, climbing a mountain, or painting a house, the key to achievement is your ability to break down the task into manageable pieces and knock them off one at one time. Focus on accomplishing what's right in front of you at this moment. Ignore what's off in the distance someplace. Substitute real-time positive thinking for negative future visualization. That's the first all- important technique for bringing an end to procrastination.

Suppose I were to ask you if you could write a 400-page novel. If you're like most people, that would sound like an impossible task. But suppose I ask you a different question. Suppose I ask if you can write a page and a quarter a day for one year. Do you think you could do it? Now, the task is starting to seem more manageable. We're breaking down the 400-page book into bite-size pieces. Even so, I suspect many people would still find the prospect intimidating. Do you know why? Writing a page and a quarter may not seem so bad, but you're being asked to look ahead one whole year. When people start to look that far ahead, many of them automatically go into a negative mode. So, let me formulate the idea of writing a book in yet another way. Let me break it down even more.

Suppose I were to ask you: Can you fill up a page and a quarter with words—not for a year, not for a month, not even for a week, but just today? Don't look any further ahead than that. I believe most people would confidently declare that they could accomplish that. Of course, these would be the same people who feel totally incapable of writing a whole book.

If I said the same thing to those people tomorrow—if I told them, I don't want you to look back, and I don't want you to look ahead, I just want you to fill up a page and a quarter this very day—do you think they could do it?

One day at a time. We've all heard that phrase. That's what we're doing here. We're breaking down the time required for a major task into one-day segments, and we're breaking down the work involved in writing a 400-page book into page-and-a-quarter increments.

Keep this up for one year, and you'll write the book. Discipline yourself to look neither forward nor backward, and you can accomplish things you never thought you could possibly do. And it all begins with those three words: break it down.

My second technique for defeating procrastination is also only three words long. The three words are: Write it down.

We know how important writing is to goal setting. The writing you'll do for beating procrastination is very similar. Instead of focusing on the future, however, you're now going to be writing about the present just as you experience it every day. Instead of describing the things you want to do or the places you want to go, you're going to describe what you actually do with your time, and you're going to keep a written record of the places you actually go.

In other words, you're going to keep a diary of your activities. And you're going to be surprised by the distractions, detours, and downright wastes of time you engage in during the course of a day. All of these get in the way of achieving your goals. For many people, it's almost like they planned it that way, and maybe at some unconscious level they did. The great thing about keeping a time diary is that it brings all this out in the open. It forces you to see what you're actually doing... and what you're not doing.

The time diary doesn't have to be anything elaborate. Just buy a little spiral notebook that you can easily carry in your pocket. When you go to lunch, when you drive across town, when you go to the dry cleaners, when you spend some time shooting the breeze at the copying machine, make a quick note of the time you began the activity and the time it ends. Try to make this notation as soon as possible; if it's inconvenient to do it immediately, you can do it later. But you should make an entry in your time diary at least once every 30 minutes, and you should keep this up for at least a week.

Break it down. Write it down. These two techniques are very straightforward. But don't let that fool you; these are powerful and effective productivity techniques that allow you put an end to procrastination and help you get started to achieving your goals.

MAKE TIME YOUR ALLY. OVER TIME YOUR TRUE CHARACTER WILL BE REVEALED BY THE CLARITY OF YOUR CONVICTIONS, THE CHOICES YOU MAKE, AND THE PROMISES YOU KEEP. HOLD STRONGLY TO YOUR PRINCIPLES AND REFUSE TO FOLLOW THE CURRENTS OF CONVENIENCE.

BUT, ACCUMULATE ENOUGH MONEY AND YOU WON'T NEED TO WORRY ABOUT ANY OF THAT NONSENSE.

Buck's Coach suggested he be more polite to large, angry customers, become better organized and manage his time better. But Buck figured that she was just over-coaching.

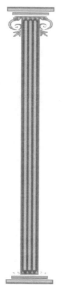

Diane M. Ruebling is president of The Ruebling Group LLC, a consulting firm that provides executive coaching, action learning team facilitation, business planning and performance systems. Her successful financial services leadership background and professional training make her consulting relevant and results oriented. Prior to starting her own company, Diane held leadership roles in various financial services companies, including national field vice president for the MONY Group and group vice president for American Express Financial Advisors. Diane can be reached at 480-248-6149 (Arizona office), 218-682-2027 (Minnesota office) or via e-mail at diane@rueblinggroup.com. Visit the Ruebling Group LLC at www.rueblinggroup.com.

Chapter Nine

525,600 MINUTES…
A YEAR IN THE LIFE OF A LEADER

Diane M. Ruebling

The bad news is that time flies.
The good news is you're the pilot.
— *Michael Alshuler*

Most leaders are on a continual quest for better time management. In this fast-paced world, you are asked to do more with less and in half the time. A typical week includes recruiting appointments, training sessions, one on ones with key people, and marketing meetings, all as you balance compliance demands. Just when you swear there is just no more time … boom! Another urgent project or task finds its way into your in-box. And the beat goes on.

So, how can a leader get ahead and start managing the schedule instead of being managed by it? Let's start by looking at (and discarding) some time management myths.

Ditch These Time Management Myths
Myth One: You Can Manage Time

One of the greatest myths is that you can manage time. How can that be? Time is. Time exists. The truth is that you can't manage time, but you *can* manage yourself in relation to time. You are the pilot of your life and, therefore, in control of the 1,440 minutes in a day and the 525,600 minutes in a year.

I recently saw an article titled "How to Have an Extra Hour a Day!" We all know that's not possible. With only a finite amount of time in a day, you need to look at effectively managing yourself in relation to that time.

Myth Two: Finding the Right Time Management Tool Will Solve Your Time Issues

People spend hundreds of millions every year buying time management systems, PDA's, calendars and other tools to solve their time management issues. These tools can be of great assistance and do have an important role, if used correctly. However, each one of these tools is marketed as a panacea that will take care of all of your time issues.

In fact, sometimes these tools can make things worse. PDA sales have increased by 32 percent this past year. Having your calendar, task list, e-mail and phone in one place can be very helpful. But people can become focused on catching every e-mail and phone message or on watching the stock market or their favorite sports team. At this point, the tool controls them. Their involvement with this time management tool actually dissipates time and deflects their focus from important tasks.

Myth Three:
The Busier You Are, the More You Get Done

Heightened periods of intensity are necessary for managers and can be beneficial for setting up a can-do atmosphere of high achievement. However, some individuals get addicted to crisis management. It keeps their adrenaline going. They like projecting an image of being in demand, necessary, or important. Leaders who believe this spend their time solving crises, accomplishing tasks and taking meetings, but not necessarily doing what is most important. They don't have systems in place or the personal discipline to make sure they spend time on what is most important, not just on what is urgent. Busy, especially frenetically busy, does not connote productivity.

Myth Four:
Planning Takes More Time

This is a convenient excuse for someone who doesn't like to plan. Research shows the opposite: *planning saves time.* Figuring out your most important tasks and activities and scheduling time blocks for them will help you be more productive and save you time in the long run.

Pareto's Principle (the 80/20 rule) says that 20 percent of your activities or tasks will produce 80 percent of your impact/productivity. Without planning, you could easily miss giving the necessary attention and time to your most important activities.

Plan to Accomplish Your Critical Activities

Okay, now that we have some of those unhelpful myths out of the way, let's rethink how you approach your daily activities.

Create a Plan

One of my favorite sayings is, "You don't climb Mt. Everest by wandering around." You also won't be successful in your career or as a leader by wandering around. You need a plan, and it is best if it is a concise plan.

Too many leaders have business plans that are huge exercises in documentation. These plans end up collecting dust on a shelf and are pulled out only at year's end, when it is time to write another plan. What will really help you in your year's journey is a document that clearly states what your vision, mission, strategies, measurable objectives, and projects are. This can be done in one page. The more concise you are, the more clear you will be. Preparing this kind of plan will increase your ability to focus yourself and your time on what matters most.

Define Your Critical Tasks

You may always be busy, but are you always working on matters that really deserve your attention? There is an exercise where someone is asked to put big rocks, pebbles, sand and water in a vase. It doesn't take long to figure out that if you don't put the big rocks in first, the vase will fill up with pebbles, sand and water. There will be no room for the big rocks. You can perform the same exercise with your day, especially as work tends to expand to fill the time available. What are your big rocks (critical tasks), pebbles (important tasks), sand (less important tasks) and water (activities of questionable value)? Figure out what your critical tasks are and then allocate blocks of time to devote to them.

One of the best ways for leaders to ensure they are allotting time for their critical tasks is to develop a model week. Imagine an audit of your calendar and your most important objectives. Would the results reflect an alignment of the two? If not, is it any wonder that you feel, despite hours and hours at the office, that you are not accomplishing what you need to?

You may need to track your time for a week or two before you develop your model week. As you review the results, you will begin to see how easy it is to be swallowed up in less important tasks, leaving less focus, capacity, and energy for your most important tasks.

In addition to helping you achieve your mission-critical goals, making better use of your time can have personal benefits, as well. Most leaders will tell you that they value work-life balance. By building a model week, they can accomplish their most important work objectives *and* have family, exercise, or vacation time. One senior vice president I know is excellent at this. He starts his days very early, especially on Thursdays, so he can leave early to go to his daughter's soccer games. He also has a date night with his wife once every two weeks. Once these items were scheduled, they happened. If you're waiting for the *right* day to get up early to work out or to leave early for a child's game, it will be hit or miss.

Determine What Activities Accomplish the Critical Tasks

I know a manager who said she never had time to accomplish her recruiting activities. One of my favorite leadership principles is:

$$Results = Activity \times Effectiveness$$

If you never do the activity in the first place, your effectiveness at it doesn't matter, and you'll never get the results you want. For this manager to accomplish her critical task, she needed to allot time each week to that activity.

One of the things that helped this manager was the model week just mentioned. A great way to confirm that you have an ideal model week is to check whether you have blocked time for the critical, high-payoff activities throughout your week. To execute these activities most effectively, these times should occur when you have the highest energy and focus. Also, allow buffer time between appointments to recalibrate and to accommodate the unexpected.

Manage Your Environment

Now that you have redefined your relationship to time, let's look at your environment to ensure it is structured to support you.

Communicate Your Priorities

Your new approach to managing your critical tasks won't work unless you communicate it to your staff and associates. You need to ask for their support in carrying out your plan and model week. The trap that many leaders fall into is being distracted by the flavor of the month, the fire of the day, or something that looks easier or is more appealing than tackling the critical tasks. Develop your team's ability to prioritize effectively and to respect the focus you have outlined. Don't forget that your assistant will be your biggest ally in your quest to manage yourself in relation to time.

Be Accessible — On Your Terms

Many leaders view their role as being available and accessible to everyone, especially if there is a crisis or need. Bona-fide, drop-everything crises do occur, but often what people call a crisis is a problem that needs attention, but not immediately. Sometimes, the problem doesn't even need *your* attention.

How many times do you hear, "Do you have a minute?" or "Can I ask a quick question?" Figure out how you want to consistently respond to these time traps in a way that is supportive and yet allows you to stay on track and focused.

Every day should have a block of time to deal with issues that come up unexpectedly or to be available to people in your organization. For instance, you could say, "Let's talk at 3:30. We can discuss it then." Frequently, the problem is resolved by the time you were supposed to meet.

Scheduling one-on-one meetings with your direct reports is a good way to avoid impromptu interruptions and requests, especially if you use an agenda. When he or she adds an item to the agenda, your subordinate has to think about whether it deserves your time and attention. Like planning, these meetings will save you time in the long run and make your organization more productive.

Schedule Brief Meetings with Planned Agendas

Meetings can be necessary and productive, but you have to manage them, too, or they can be a huge time trap. Some organizations get caught up in having meetings for everything. Economist John Kenneth Galbraith once quipped, "Meetings are indispensable when you don't want to do anything." To make sure that doesn't happen, conduct meetings with clear agendas and defined outcomes. Create the expectation that participants will come to meetings prepared. Have someone facilitate so you stay on the agenda. Pursuing tangents ends up lengthening the meeting and decreasing everyone's focus.

A popular concept is to have short power or stand-up meetings. For instance, to make sure that everyone is focused on the right activities for the day, have a 10-minute stand-up meeting each morning. When standing, people will get to the point and be more focused, more so than when they settle into their chair at the conference table with a cup of coffee. Another time enhancer is to have meetings at the end of the day or right before lunch. People will be more likely to press for results, knowing they have other commitments.

Leap Forward

So what will your new week look like? Well, your day will still be filled with activity. However, instead of feeling frustrated that you're never getting to the big stuff or that you haven't had the chance to have the impact that you want, you'll feel calmer and be more effective. You'll be spending your time where it really counts: on the activities that you know will bring you the biggest return. You'll still be available to staff and associates, but within boundaries. The planning that you have done—from the macro strategic level to the micro meeting level—allows everyone to focus on what is important, not just on what flew in the door that day.

The final step for making this vision come true is to commit to change and believe in your power to change. Without those two things, in fact, none of these ideas or suggestions will work. The road to fully unleashing the power to succeed starts with your personal commitment.

As you attempt to change how you and your organization plan and schedule activities, don't become frustrated. Remember that leadership is what you do for a living. Make some decisions about managing yourself in relation to time, commit to them and leap forward to your new reality.

Key Strategies: Make Your Time Count

- You can't manage time; you *can* manage yourself in relation to time.

- Manage your schedule and activities to accomplish your critical tasks.

- Start with planning. How else will you know what tasks are critical to accomplishing your goals?

- Your model week should include blocks of time devoted to the activities necessary to accomplish your critical tasks. If you're not performing the activity, how can you hope to win?

- Communicate your priorities to staff and associates. Be accessible, but within boundaries.

- Use power meetings, agendas, and facilitators to enjoy useful, focused, and *short* meetings.

- Make a conscious decision to change your time management habits and commit to it.

*"Finish every day and be done with it
you have done what you could;
some blunders and absurdities crept in.
Forget them as soon as you can.
Tomorrow is a new day;
you shall begin it serenely and with too
high a spirit to be encumbered with
your old nonsense...*

--Ralph Waldo Emerson

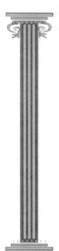 **Brian Tracy** is the most listened to audio author on personal and business success in the world today. He is the author/narrator of countless best-selling audio learning programs and the author of 16 books. All rights reserved worldwide. Copyright © 2006. Contact Brian Tracy at:

Brian Tracy International
462 Stevens Ave., Suite 202
Solana Beach, CA 92075
Phone: (858) 481-2977
www.BrianTracy.com

Chapter Ten

MANAGING YOUR TIME

Brian Tracy

Perhaps the greatest single problem that people have today is "time poverty." Working people have too much to do and too little time for their personal lives. Most people feel overwhelmed with responsibilities and activities; and the harder they work, the farther behind they feel. This sense of being on a never-ending treadmill can cause you to fall into the reactive/responsive mode of living. Instead of clearly deciding what you want to do, you continually react to what is happening around you. Pretty soon, you lose all sense of control. You feel that your life is running you, rather than you running your life.

On a regular basis, you have to stand back and take stock of yourself and what you're doing. You have to stop the clock and do some serious thinking about who you are and where you are going. You have to evaluate your activities in the light of what is really important to you. You must master your time, rather than becoming a slave to the constant flow of events and demands on your time. And you must organize your life to achieve balance, harmony, and inner peace. Taking action without thinking is the cause of every failure. Your ability to think is the most valuable trait that you possess. If you improve the quality of your thinking, you improve the quality of your life, sometimes immediately.

Time is your most precious resource. It is the most valuable thing you have. It is perishable, it is irreplaceable, and it cannot be saved. It can only be reallocated from activities of lower value to activities of higher value. All work requires time, and time is absolutely essential for the important relationships in your life. The very act of taking a moment to think about your time before you spend it will begin to improve your personal time management immediately.

I used to think that time management was only a business tool, like a calculator or a cellular telephone. It was something that you used so that you could get more done in a shorter period of time and eventually be paid more money. Then I learned that time management is not a peripheral activity or skill. It is the core skill upon which everything else in life depends.

In your work or business life, there are so many demands on your time from other people that very little of your time is yours to use as you choose. However, at home and in your personal life, you can exert a tremendous amount of control over how you use your time. It is in this area that I want to focus.

Personal time management begins with you. It begins with your thinking through what is really important to you in life. It only makes sense if you organize it around specific things that you want to accomplish. You need to set goals in three major areas of your life. First, you need family and personal goals. These are the reasons why you get up in the morning, why you work hard and upgrade your skills, why you worry about money and sometimes feel frustrated by the demands on your time.

What are your personal and family goals, both tangible and intangible? A tangible family goal could be a bigger house, a better car, a larger television set, a vacation, or anything else that costs money. An intangible goal would be to build a higher quality relationship with your spouse and children or to spend more time with your family, going for walks or reading books. Achieving these family and personal goals are the real essence of time management and its major purpose.

The second area is your business and career goals. These are the "how" goals, the means by which you achieve your personal "why" goals. How can you achieve the level of income that will enable you to fulfill your family goals? How can you develop the skills and abilities to stay ahead of the curve in your career? Business and career goals are absolutely essential, especially when balanced with family and personal goals.

The third type of goals are your personal development goals. Remember, you can't achieve much more on the outside than what you have achieved on the inside. Your outer life will be a reflection of your inner life. If you wish to achieve worthwhile things in your personal and career life, you must become a worthwhile person in your own self-development. You must build yourself if you want to build your life. Perhaps the greatest secret of success is that you can become anything you really want to become to achieve any goal that you really want to achieve. But, in order to do it, you must go to work on yourself and never stop.

Once you have a list of your personal and family goals, your business and career goals, and your self-development goals, you can then organize the list by priority. This brings us to the difference between priorities and posteriorities. In order to get your personal time under control, you must very clearly decide your priorities. You must decide the most important things that you could possibly be doing to give yourself the same amount of happiness, satisfaction, and joy in life. But at the same time, you must establish posteriorities, as well. Just as priorities are things that you do more of and sooner, posteriorities are things that you do less of and later.

The fact is, your calendar is full. You have no spare time. Your time is extremely valuable. Therefore, for you to do anything new, you will have to stop doing something old. In order to get into something, you will have to get out of something else. In order to pick something up, you will have to put something down. Before you make any new commitment of your time, you must firmly decide what activities you are going to discontinue in your personal life. If you want to spend more time with your family, for example, you must decide what activities you currently engage in that are preventing you from doing so.

A principle of time management says that hard time pushes out soft time. This means that hard time, such as working, will push out soft time, such as the time you spend with your family. If you don't get your work done at the office because you don't use your time well, you almost invariably have to rob that time from your family. As a result, because your family is important to you, you find yourself in a values conflict. You feel stressed and irritable. You feel a tremendous amount of pressure. You know in your heart that you should be spending more time with the important people in your life, but because you didn't get your work done, you have to fulfill those responsibilities before you can spend time with your spouse and children.

Think of it this way. Every minute you waste during the waking day is time that your family will ultimately be deprived of. So, concentrate on working when you are at work so that you can concentrate on your family when you are at home.

There are three key questions that you can continually ask yourself to keep your personal life in balance. The first question is, "What is really important to me?" Whenever you find yourself with too much to do and too little time, stop and ask yourself, "What is it that is really important for me to do in this situation?" Then, make sure that what you are doing is the answer to that question.

The second question is, "What are my highest value activities?" In your personal life, this means, "What are the things that I do that give me the greatest pleasure and satisfaction? Of all the things that I could be doing at any one time, what are the things that I could do to add the greatest value to my life?"

And the final question for you to ask over and over again is, "What is the most valuable use of my time right now?" Since you can only do one thing at a time, you must constantly organize you life so that you are doing one thing, the most important thing, at every moment. Personal time management enables you to choose what to do first, what to do second, and what not to do at all. It enables you to organize every aspect of your life so that you can get the greatest joy, happiness, and satisfaction out of everything you do.

"An unhurried sense of time is in itself a form of wealth."
- Bonnie Friedman

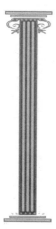

Debra J. Satterwhite, ABR, Systems Designer and Spiritual Director, has been working in the real estate field since 1976. She is a Real Estate Consultant in Northern California and designs "systems" for real estate professionals. Debra completed her Spiritual Direction training at the Spiritual Director's Institute, Burlingame, California and is a member of Spiritual Directors International.

Contact Debra at debras@nccn.net or telephone (530) 277-7568.

Chapter Eleven

TIME MANAGEMENT – TIPS AND TRICKS

Debra J. Satterwhite

The Four R's – Remember, Record, Routine, Reward

The statement "time management" has always seemed a bit odd to me. Time can't be managed. It simply is. The only thing we have control of is what we decide to do with the 1,440 minutes we have in a day. What we do in those 1,440 minutes will determine if we are fulfilled or simply existing.

As described by the Greeks, there are two types of time – kronos and kairos. Kronos time is how we typically describe time – linear, measured, and tracked by a clock. Kairos time is when we are so absorbed in an activity or feeling that we "lose track of time." It is my belief that a person living a fulfilled life knows the importance of both kronos and kairos time.

Living a fulfilled life includes learning and using time management to minimize effort and maximize results. **Remember**, **record**, **routine** and **reward** is my formula for actualizing this equation.

Remember

The first step is to **remember**. Remember what your goals are. What is your overall vision for this "chapter" of your life? Without this information, any attempt at time management will be futile and unproductive. Set goals for the calendar year and then break each goal down to projects, action plans, activities, and timelines. Then, prepare timelines and activities for your months, weeks and days. **TIP: Write down your dreams and goals clearly.**

In January of each year, I attend a Women's Visioning Circle. The day is designed to help me look at what things in my life I'm ready to let go of, who I want to be a year from now, and the real purpose of my life and goal setting. I set goals for career, health, creativity, family-home, leisure, relationship, prosperity, spirituality, and self.

At the end of this visioning day, each attendee stands in front of the group and speaks from the internal place of having already accomplished the goals just formulated. The "circle of women" affirms the woman speaking and lifts up the desires and goals to the world. This exercise is one of the most empowering activities I do each year. This day is kairos time.

My goal sheet hangs in my personal room at home for the entire year. Each time I step into this room, I see my goals. I am forced to **remember** what it is I want to accomplish. **TRICK: Remember what it is you want—the first step to effective time management.**

Record

Record means write it down. The initial "writing it down" happens when you write out your annual dreams and goals (or a five year plan, ten year plan, etc.). It is not the same to think about your goals as it is to write them down. This ritual has been proven over time to work. Don't question why; just do it.

The "**record**" I want to delve into here is how you manifest those dreams and goals in reality. It comes down to a daily list of things to do.

TIP: Make a list of what you want to do each day. There are two schools of thought on this. Make the list the night before. If it is work related, you make your list for tomorrow the very last thing before you leave the office. If it is personal, you could write it out just before you go to bed.

My dad always told me that when he had a problem to solve at work, he would register it in his subconscious at bedtime, asking his mind to find the answer while he slept. It worked for him all the time. Ever notice when you wake up in the wee hours of the morning, you get some of your best ideas and most clever ways of working something out? You have probably been mulling it around in your brain for days trying to access the best solution(s). Sleeping can be good for more than physical rest.

This working of the subconscious is a good reason to make the list the night before. The other reason is that it will minimize your "mind chatter." If you've written it all down, the mind doesn't have to worry about remembering it and is free to focus on other things (i.e., your children, your spouse, yourself, etc.).

The other option is to make the list first thing in the morning. The important thing is to make the list. Experiment with both and see what works best for you.

I make my list on white, lined pads and write it out in longhand. Put your list on the kind of paper (or electronic format) that works for you. I'm visual. I like to see my list on paper in front of me. I want to be able to cross out each item when it is done. Don't worry about how anyone else does it. Experiment and find out what works for you and do it.

Determine what absolutely has to get done today. Move the things you didn't accomplished yesterday to today's list. **TRICK: Don't be afraid to eliminate an item if you discover it is not productive.** Get honest—is there a chance you probably won't ever do it? Then, get rid of it. Free up the brain space.

Decide the two or three things that absolutely must get accomplished. Prioritize the list. First, I **remember** what I'm trying to accomplish. Then, what activity will go direct to my "bottom line." Lastly, I write down 1, 2, 3, etc., in the left hand margin next to each item.

TIP: Do the most difficult thing and/or the thing you like the least first. Get it out of your brain space and out of the way. You know it. I know you know it. You will feel so good when it is done, and the momentum will carry you through the day. Don't be fooled by doing a bunch of the "little stuff" on the list because the items are "easy" and "won't take much time." You know how it goes . . . the phone rings, another project comes up, an emergency happens. Yes, some little stuff got done, and you "crossed off" some stuff, but the real priority hasn't even been touched. **TIP: Even the best planned day must have room for interruptions and emergencies; don't expect to get everything on the list done. Prioritize!**

Experiment and decide how you want to record your daily list. **TRICK: Stop worrying about how everyone else does it and honor yourself.** You have permission to work the way that serves you best. Figure it out, own it, and stick to it.

This brings me to the next "R."

Routine

Writing out your annual dreams and goals is a **routine**. Breaking them down to projects, action plans, activities, and timelines is a **routine**. Doing a prioritized, daily list of things to do is a **routine.** Doing "the most difficult thing or the thing you like the least the first" is a **routine**. Routine is kronos time.

A **routine** is setting up "systems," if you will, that work for you. **Routine** is the way you work. It is the way you manifest your goals and dreams. **Routine** helps manage your life with minimum effort and maximum results.

TIP: Make focus time a routine. Focus time is when you allow yourself a period of time with no interruptions. I mean that literally – no answering the phone, no checking e-mail, not text messaging, no human interactions. This allows you to focus totally on the most productive item on your daily list (remember to do the most difficult thing or thing you like least first).

For some, this may seem like a luxury. It is not. It is imperative. Company owners must insist on it for themselves and for their employees. The amount of work produced by someone is directly correlated to how proficient they are at focus time.

TRICK: Set a timer for a specified period of focus time. An appointment reminder feature, computer timer, a PDA alarm all work. I use a kitchen timer. I have one on my desk at the office and at home. You accomplish two things by setting a timer: 1) You will have total focus on the project in front of you – freed up brain space. You will get the project done more quickly, more creatively and do a better job, and 2) You will never be late for an appointment or meeting.

Part of a good routine is self care including exercise, good food, leisure activities, etc. **TIP: Remember to include something each day that feeds your soul, mind, and body and points you in the direction of the true purpose for your life.** This is no easy task and requires self examination, self knowledge, and raw honesty. It is worth the effort. If you don't know what this looks like for you, my suggestion is to make it one your annual goals.

TIP: **Allow a day(s) in the week with no routine.**
Consistent, strict routine with no breaks, while productive,
can become tedious and annoying. On the "no routine"
day, be creative with what you want the day to feel like
and look like. Let yourself simply "be." **TRICK: Step in
kairos time whenever possible.**

And, when I mention kairos time, I think reward.

Reward

What can you do for yourself if you get your "to do" list
for the day completed? What will you do for yourself if
you complete a project? What will you do for yourself if
you reach a major goal you have set for yourself?

Reward is an important piece for me. It helps keep me
focused, on task, and motivated. Rewards come in many
forms and don't have to cost money. Some rewards cost a
little money and others a lot of money. I like to spend
"reward" in kairos time. **TRICK: Make the reward
personal and truly enjoyable – know what motivates you.**
I'm a movie buff. You want to see me zip through my list
of things to do for the day? First thing I do is make the list.
Then, I go on-line and find out what time the movie starts
that I want to see. Whoola . . . I eat up my list in record
time. Some days, I don't need a "reward." Some days, I
do.

This reward piece of the Four R's is about knowing
yourself really well. It's about being honest with yourself
at the start of the day. Some days, I'm simply "on." I don't
need anything to motivate me. Yippee. Good for me!

Some days, if I'm really honest with myself, I simply know I'm going to have to set myself up with a reward if I'm going to accomplish anything.

What would be a reward worth working toward for you? What will get your soul singing and put you in kairos time? Leaving the office early and picking up the kids from school and taking them out for an ice cream? Reading a novel? Writing a novel? Going for a hike? Tinkering in the garage? A massage? Here again, you must know yourself. **TIP: You must figure out what "fun" means to you and then actually give yourself permission to enjoy it.**

Here is a word about vacations. **TIP: Vacations are not a reward, but a necessity.** The body, mind, and soul need time to regenerate. My mentors and coaches have taught me to put my vacations on the calendar FIRST. I literally mean the first day, or within the first week, of the new year. Once you have determined the vacation dates, then put in work, charity, etc.

There are "extended" vacations—a week, two weeks, month, a six-month sabbatical. Get them on the calendar. Decide what will serve you best on these very precious days. If you have a family to consider, then make plans accordingly. If at all possible, plan some time for yourself...even if it is one afternoon of the family vacation.

And here again, be honest. What is your idea of a vacation? Is it horizontal with a book or clipped to a "zip line" in the jungle? Or is it a combination of both? This is a very important discussion to have with your spouse, children or others with whom you plan to spend your vacation time. **TRICK: Communicate your vacation expectations; make this precious time a win-win.**

How about a "mini vacation" – one 24-hour period off with no phone, voice mail, pager, PDA—no electronics whatsoever, or a 2 to 3 day period off? My idea of a mini vacation is to wake up in the morning, start a book I've dying to read, and stay in bed until I've read the whole thing. What would be your idea of a mini vacation?

Having commented on the necessity of vacation, it can also be used as a reward. Maybe where you go or what you do on your vacation can be the added "reward" factor. If the prospect of a certain type of vacation is a motivator for you, then by all means use it in that way.

Reward is an integral part of minimizing effort and maximizing production.

The Four "R's"

Where to start? You are probably already proficient at several of the Four R's. Consider choosing the "R" you would find most difficult or like the least – start there.

The important thing is to do something. One of my coaches, Kathy Courtney, always says, "I don't care **what** you decide; I care **that** you decide." These are words I'll never forget and say to myself often.

Remember your dreams and goals. **Record** how you want to get there – the big picture and the day to day. Build a **Routine** that works for you. **Reward** yourself.

It's your life…enjoy it!

*"You can't change the past,
but you can ruin the present by worrying
about the future."*
- Author Unknown

Although Lucy hadn't worked in the corporate environment for some time, she was confident that her time management and organizational skills would carry the day.

MEET OUR CARTOONISTS

Germaine Porche´, MSOD and Jed Niederer CLU have successfully coached and consulted executives, teams and entrepreneurs in accelerating business performance internationally for more than 18 years. They have led workshops on leadership, breakthrough performance, communication, coaching, and personal and organizational effectiveness for more than 100,000 people in 15 countries.

Germaine and Jed co-authored *Coach Anyone About Anything: How to Help People Succeed in Business and Life,* which was listed among Amazon's Best 100 Business Books of 2003. Their new bestseller, *Coaching Soup for the Cartoon Soul,* points at the lighter side of Business and Life Coaching through their original cartoons, while highlighting useful coaching principles and concepts.

The American Business Women's Association named Germaine one of the *Top Ten Businesswomen in America* for ABWA for 2006.

Jed earned degrees in Communications and Advertising from the University of Washington in Seattle, WA, and a Chartered Life Underwriter (CLU) degree from The American College in Bryn Mawr, PA. They can be reached at jed@eaglesview.com or gporche@eaglesview.com Telephone: 888-387-9786 or visit: www.eaglesview.com.

Chapter Twelve

THE MAGIC OF GENERATING TIME!

Germaine Porché and Jed Niederer

Technological innovations allow us to instantly have commands and controls at our fingertips. In a moment's notice, you can communicate to a large mass of people just by pressing the send button in your email program. Things are moving by so rapidly, and we're able to access more all at once that we're consumed with accomplishing and doing more. This is exciting and, yet, how often do we wish we had the witchery powers of Samantha, accomplishing more in less time with the twitch of our nose?

The Notion of Saving Time

In our desire to get more accomplished, we search for ways to "save time," to squeeze more into our already busy schedules. Germaine enjoys running marathons. When she first started training, she experienced some frustration from adding her daily run to her schedule. In her quest to "save time," she realized that she couldn't run any faster than her body would let her. Saving time was an illusion. You cannot "save time." Yet, we hear the notion that you can save time regularly. "Save time here," "save time there." Actually, there is no such thing as "saving time!"

In fact, the notion that we can save time keeps us less powerful and a bit naive with regard to the phenomenon we call "time."

You simply cannot save time like a thing or commodity. You cannot <u>bank</u> time. You cannot bank "now." If there was a *time bank,* to explore the analogy a little further, your account has a <u>finite balance</u> for which you cannot get an accurate statement. You have unstoppable, automatic withdrawals! You spend a day, everyday, no matter what. There's no saving time. Each and every week has 168 hours in it, and you can never get it back. You use it or lose it!

> *"Yesterday is a canceled check;*
> *tomorrow is a promissory note;*
> *<u>today</u> is the only cash you have - so spend it wisely."*
> Kay Lyons, author

Now, we have said that you cannot save time, but we didn't say that there weren't things that you can do to capture time and make the time invested more productive. In fact, in a certain sense, you can "generate" time.

Time is Pretty Potent Stuff

As a practice, Jed and I make a game of looking for ways to get more done or to fit more into a block of time. It's a great way to *generate* time! For example, we were driving to see a movie early one evening and noticed that we had about 15 minutes to spare. The little chatterbox in my head took this opportunity to remind me that I needed a speakerphone! "Ah ha!" I said, "Let's go for it, Jed! Whad'ya say?" "Whew, 15 minutes, I don't know,

Germaine. There are so many different types of phones and features to choose from...," Jed said. "Jed, it's a game, remember? We can get the phone <u>and</u> make the movie on time. <u>Let's generate some time!</u> **Pull in here!**" So, we parked the car and ran into the closest store in the mall that sold telephones. We rapidly selected the speakerphone I wanted, paid the cashier and dashed for the movie. We arrived at the movie early, with enough time to get popcorn and drinks; and the next morning I had my regularly scheduled one-hour coaching conference call. And that morning, I suffered no "telephone ear" from the handset!

Generating time is a great game and can pay enormous dividends. One of the big benefits is that playing this game instantly moves you away from being a "time victim." We are all *time victims* to some degree. You know you're being a *time victim* whenever you say you can't have, do, or be something because of time.

Routine Actions –
A Great Source of Time Generation

A number of years ago when Jed was in the insurance business, his friend, Ted, made a lasting contribution to him. Ted noticed how incredibly slow Jed was at getting dressed in the morning to go to work.

They were staying at a hotel and had overslept. The "wake up call" never came. To make matters even more exciting, their ride to the home office was the Agency Vice President, Stephen. They thought, with some reason, that it might be "bad form" to make Steve wait. Anyway, Ted was dressed in no time and marveled at how slow Jed was. Ted said, "Jed, will you hurry up! Steve's waiting downstairs for us. Move it!" He said other equally motivating things, and they finally made it downstairs. In Steve's car on the way to the office, Ted was telling Steve the story and said, "Jed's only got one speed in the morning, SLOW."

Well, that made an impact on Jed. He examined his morning routine. He discovered that he held the belief that it took at least an hour for him to shave, shower, and get dressed. He inquired of other men how long they needed for this daily ritual. Jed discovered that, on average, he took twice as long as everyone he interviewed. Thunderbolt! If he could invest just 15 minutes less every morning in this activity, he reasoned, he would generate more than 90 hours a year to invest elsewhere (91 and ¼ hours to be exact). That represents nearly <u>two work weeks</u> for most of us! And it is high-quality morning hours, to boot! (Jed works most effectively in the morning.) So, he set out to change his routine.

Jed conceived of the idea to make routines, like getting dressed in the morning, "Athletic Events!" That's right, athletic events. He even bought a stop-watch for this purpose. He shaved off seconds and minutes every day until he got getting dressed down to 22 minutes flat! That amounts to 38 minutes that he generates every day. That's 231.16 high-value hours per year or the equivalent of almost 6 work weeks! Or, he can invest the time in vacations, tennis, golf, etc. How much time can you generate from routine actions?

Time Traditions –
Breathe New Life into Old Activities

This breakthrough discovery led us to examine all sorts of routines. We have named this discovery, "time traditions." Time traditions are the personal habits we have with regard to regular activities that consume blocks of time. These traditions can be personal, as well as cultural. Corporate cultures can harbor many unproductive time traditions. There are traditional meeting lengths, traditional meeting frequencies, traditional meeting times, traditional conference call lengths, traditional meeting locations, and the list goes on and on. We even have traditional vacation times! Unexamined and unconscious time traditions rob thousands of people precious time that could be more wisely invested in their lives!

Remember, just fifteen recaptured minutes in your day are about two work weeks in one year. What could you produce with two extra weeks this year?

On the following page is the Time Traditions exercise from our Eagle's View Time Transformation Course:

EXERCISE:

1. On the following page, <u>add to the list</u> of time traditions with your own.

2. <u>Change the example time figures</u> next to the time traditions already listed <u>to match your own personal experience</u>.

3. After you have exhausted all of the "time traditions" you can think of, go back and challenge the numbers.

   a. Estimate how much time you could be committed to shave off of each time tradition.

   b. Multiply each of the "shavings" by the approximate number of times you participate in this activity in a year's time. For example, 20 minutes x 52 weeks = 1,040 minutes or 17.3 hours.

   c. Calculate the total time you could possibly generate in one year, to invest elsewhere.

4. Pick yourself up off of the floor and go to it!

Time Traditions

What do you traditionally invest?

What's Possible?

☐ Lunch _____ 1 hour ____
☐ Sleep _____ 8 hours ____
☐ Dinner _____ 1 ½ hours ____
☐ Meetings _____ ½, 1 hour ____
☐ Conference Calls ____ 1 hour ____
☐ Dressing _____ ¾ hour ____
☐ Breakfast _____ ½ hour ____
☐ _____ _____ ____
☐ _____ _____ ____
☐ _____ _____ ____
☐ _____ _____ ____
☐ _____ _____ ____
☐ _____ _____ ____
☐ _____ _____ ____
☐ _____ _____ ____
☐ _____ _____ ____

Generating Time as a Practice

Another thing we've developed that has proven to be extremely useful is this Time Generator Checklist. We carry it permanently on a printed card for frequent review.

TIME GENERATOR CHECKLIST

a) What do I do regularly that I can stop doing altogether or delegate?

b) What meetings can I eliminate or cut the time spent by 25%? 50%? 75%?

c) When people drop in on you, tell them how much time you have to speak with them and stick to it.

d) What trips (travel) can I eliminate or delegate? (43% of people find delegating difficult.)

e) What opportunities do I see in my schedule where I can get additional things done at the same event?

f) Who on my staff can I develop to do the things that I "believe" that only I can do now?

g) What routine processes should I "checklist" to save mental energy for myself and my staff?

h) Am I stuck in any time traditions?

We are not presenting this list as the last word on generating time. To the contrary, this list is by no means complete. In fact, <u>we invite you to add to the list and to personalize it to meet your own special needs</u>. People have told us that they have added things like, "What am I being too significant about and not getting into action? Who's doing my prioritizing today, me or my company?

Where am I being a *time victim*, and what can I do about it?" One of our clients put the list on a large poster and hung it on an office wall to make a game of adding to the list for the staff. You can learn quite a lot from your staff about how to generate time. They see things you don't see.

We invite you to make a game of generating and capturing time. Have fun with it! Please don't have it be a heavy burden or chore. Experience proves that when activities are fun, people's results improve dramatically.

We wish you all the very best in your quest to generate time and multiply your desired outcomes.

"We always overestimate the change that will occur in the next two years and underestimate the change that will occur in the next ten."
- Bill Gates

Denis Waitley is a respected author, keynote speaker and productivity consultant on high performance human achievement. The following article was reproduced with permission from Denis Waitley's Weekly Ezine. To subscribe to Denis Waitley's Weekly Ezine, go to www.deniswaitley.com or send an email with the word "Join" in the subject line to subscribe@deniswaitley.com

Chapter Thirteen

BALANCE YOUR WORKLOAD WITH A GENEROUS NUMBER OF MINI-VACATIONS FOR MAXIMUM PRODUCTIVITY

Denis Waitley

By re-energizing and renewing yourself frequently, you will avoid burnout and become much more motivated and productive. Don't keep your nose to the grindstone for years and wait for retirement to travel. Balance and consistency are the keys. Enjoy the process, not just the result. Don't fight the passing of time. Don't fear it, squander it, or try to hide from it under a superficial cosmetic veil of fads and indulgences. Life and time go together. Do enjoy each phase of life. Do make the most of each day and draw maximum joy from each moment.

Many people today are concerned with quality time – time generally defined in part as that spent on recreation, personal pursuits, time with children, spouse, and friends. While I certainly believe quality time is important, I believe two other aspects of time are equally important.

First, one must also spend quantity time. The average father spends less than 30 minutes each week in direct one-on-one communication with each of his children. How can we possibly expect good family relationships with so little communication?

Second, one must spend regular time. Many supervisors and company presidents go for weeks, even months, without seeing many of their employees. There's no substitute for regular meetings and open forums in which managers and team members can share ideas.

Time has a dual structure. On one hand, we live our daily routines, meeting present contingencies as they arise. On the other hand, our most ambitious goals and desires need time so that they can be assembled and cemented. A long-term goal connects pieces of time into one block. These blocks can be imagined and projected into the future as we do when we set goals for ourselves. Or, these blocks of time can be created in retrospect as we do when we look back at what we've accomplished.

It's not in the image of our big dreams that we run the risk of losing our focus and motivation. It's the drudgery and routine of our daily lives that present the greatest danger to our hopes for achievement. Good time management means that you maximize the daily return on the energy and mental effort you expend.

Ways to maximize your time productivity:

- Write down in one place all the important contacts you have and all of your goals and priorities. Make a backup copy, preferably on CD, DVD, or Zip disc. Write down every commitment you make at the time you make it.

- Stop wasting the first hour of your workday. Having the chat and first cup of coffee, reading the paper, and socializing are the three costliest opening exercises that lower productivity.

- Do one thing well at a time. It takes time to start and stop work on each activity. Stay with a task until it is completed.

- Don't open unimportant mail. More than a fourth of the mail you receive can be tossed before you open or read it, and that includes e-mail.

- Handle each piece of paper only once and never more than twice. Don't set aside anything without taking action. Carry work, reading material, audiotapes and your laptop computer with you everywhere you go. Convert down time into uplink time.

- Spend 20 minutes at the beginning of each week and 10 minutes at the beginning of each day planning your to do list.

- Set aside personal relaxation time during the day. Don't work during lunch. It's neither noble nor nutritional to skip important energy input and stress-relieving time. Throughout the day, ask yourself, "What's the best use of my time right now?" As the day grows short, focus on projects you can least afford to leave undone.

- And, as we said at the beginning of this message, take vacations often, mini-vacations of two or three days, and leave your work at home. The harder you work, the more you need to balance your exercise and leisure time.

Action Idea: Plan a relaxing three-day vacation within the next three months without taking any business work with you. Reserve it on your calendar this week.

"You will never "find" time for anything. If you want time, you must make it."
- Charles Bruxton

Chapter Fourteen

GET ORGANIZED NOW

Machen P. MacDonald, CPCC, CCSC

Here is a news flash—there is always going to be more to do than you can do. That's just the way it is due to the speed and access of information available to us these days. So, the trick is to get off your own back and free up some of that mental RAM of yours so you can focus and be more effective at what's important to you.

So, how do you do that?

The answer is--Understand your G.P.A. to maximize your lists and don't use stacks to remind you of what needs to get done.

First, let's take a look at lists. Most people have a "To-Do" list. However, for most people, many of those daily to do's go from one day to the next, to the next, to next week, to next month and to ....oh, why bother? I will explain how to create and work with your lists effectively in a moment. But first, let me share with you some reasons why most people's organizational strategies fail them and what you can do to avoid the pitfalls.

Avoid the stacks. When I coach people, I am always curious about the stacks of stuff on their desk, credenza, or floor, or for that matter, all three. What usually happens is something is mission critical and they keep it out to remind them to take care of it. Then more stuff comes in at them. They don't know where to file it, and it ends up taking space on the desk. Pretty soon, the stacks are a repelling blend of action and reference and the client has no idea what's in the stack. All they know is there is something important buried somewhere that is creating a gnawing sense of anxiety because it is not getting done. The problem is they don't know what is not getting done.

You can actually be more effective when you know what is not getting done and consciously decide not to do it, versus not knowing what's not getting done and worrying that something important that should be getting done is not getting done. The solution is to file reference items in an A-Z filing system when they come in and to file action items in a holding file titled Actions. Then create a To Do list that corresponds with that Actions file. If you want to take this concept to the next level, I would suggest you get 31 folders—one for each day of the month and file the action items in the corresponding day that is best suited for getting that item completed. You can also get 12 more folders—one for each month of the year. Then, when something comes in and it doesn't need your attention until four months from now, you stick it in that corresponding folder, and at the beginning of that month when you need to see it, you will see it and it hasn't taken up any desk space or mental RAM during the interim. If you work this system, I guarantee you will experience more energy and time!

Besides losing track of your work in all the brain-drain stacks, here is the reason why you may not be turning your To-Do's in to "Ta Da's!" Your To-Do list is filled with more projects than actions. For a To-Do list to be effective and get completed, it must contain only action items. It also helps if they are segmented by context and time. Here's what I mean. The important thing to know is that a project has more than one action item to it. It can be as little as two or three actions. However, that's the trap. Here's why. If you don't consciously know what the next action within the project is, you will avoid engaging in the project. That's called procrastination! That's why what you think is a To-Do on your list never seems to get done, unless perhaps an emergency erupts and you have no choice but to think through the project and become consciously aware of what the next action steps are. Can you relate to this?

The way to effectively use lists to get more done in less time is to understand and apply your G.P.A. No, not your grade point average. G.P.A. stands for your Goals-Projects-Actions. If you visualize the completion of your Goals and think the process through from end to beginning, you will have a high level overview of what's needed to accomplish your goals. To achieve your goals, the completion of various projects is necessary. Projects are made up of various action items which must be completed. So, think G.P.A. Once you have thought through each of your goals and become consciously aware of the projects needed to support the achievement of those goals and the action items to support the completion of each project, you are on your way.

If you do this, you will have more energy because you are not trying to keep it all in your mental RAM. Your brain works the same way a computer does. If you open up too many files, what happens? That's right, your computer either slows down or crashes because it is using too much RAM. When you try to keep it all in your head, you are essentially doing the same thing. It is draining you of energy and efficiency. Write it or type it down on a list and free up your RAM.

Once you have identified all the single action items to do, you must segment those actions items on to your To-Do list in a way that you won't become numb to your list and not see what's on it. Here are some suggestions on how you may want to segment your list:

- Phone Calls
- Things you can only do at a computer
- WWW's to check out
- Things you can only do at the office other than at computer
- Things you can only do at home
- Books to buy
- Videos to rent
- Things to do with kids on the weekend
- Waiting For…(Things to follow up on once you have delegated them)
- Someday, Maybe…

In this way, you can scan that portion of your list and see what is the best next action to do based on what context or environment you are in and how much time you have currently to do that something on your list.

You must be somewhat aware of how much time each action should take and how much time you have available to put toward that action. You see, if you only have 15 minutes until your next appointment comes in, you are going to make a different decision of what action item to do than if you had a 2 hour block of time and your computer is down.

If you can get in the habit of taking an hour or so each Friday and updating your list, you will be amazed at how much more you can get done in the same or less amount of time than you did before. The real benefit to this system is you will not be so wiped at the end of each day or the end of the week and you can enjoy life with the important people in your life.

So when it comes to effective To-Do lists and getting results, think G.P.A., Context and Time and avoid the brain-drain stacks.

"There is time for everything."
- Thomas Edison

Tex knew full well that there was no magic wand that would alleviate his clients' time management problems.

But, they kept paying him. So, . . . "Tah dahhhhh!"

Quick Order Form

THE POWER OF COACHING SERIES

$14.95

Shipping: $4.60 for first book
$1.25 for each additional book
(California residents add 8.25% sales tax)

Fax Orders	Telephone Orders
Send this form to:	Call Toll Free:
530-687-8583	1-530-273-8000
	(With credit card ready)
Order On Line	
www.ThePowerOfCoaching.com	

Book	Quantity
• Managing the Time of Your Life	
• Engaging Excellence in Others	
• The Secrets of Achievement	

Name _____

Address:_____

City/State/Zip:_____

Phone: _____ Email: ____ _____

Method of Payment:

Visa   Master Card   American Express   Discover

Card Number:_____

Name on Card: _____

Expiration Date: _____ 3-digit security code on back of card: ____

(If billing address is different from shipping address, please provide.)

NOTES